Spitting Into
A River

Spitting Into A River

By Mary T. Altobelli

Acknowledgements

I'd like to recognize the wonderful people who collaborated with me on this project and those that encouraged me every step of the way.

First and foremost Janet Hamill for her guidance and editing. Janet is a talented poet, surrealist and mentor extrodinaire. She helped shape my fragmented stories into a solid comprehensive tale.

Thank you Jean Campbel-Galli, your understanding of my zany ideas just reinforces our ever-growing friendship.

Thank you to my daughter, Gabriella Newrock for your fabulous cover design. Thank you Marisa Genna for your editng expertise. Thank you Lia Fierro for legal advice and thank you Steve Siciliano for sharing the photos of you and Charlie. Thank you Yonkers, without you I'd have no street smarts. Thank you Peter Bliss, your belief in me keeps me true to my nature.

Thank you John Lennon, because of you I was able to afford to put my daughter through college.

Finally, thank you to all those nameless people who helped me cross over a bridge, strangers who so many years ago, picked up a hitchhiker.

We are all hitchhikers on this journey called life.

In Memory of Eleanor Javid,

who listened to my tales, inspired and encouraged me

and I suspect is still laughing.

Contents

Part 2

Prologue
Zombie Land

What exactly is Yonkers?

It is a place, a city, and the backdrop of my juvenile life. Yonkers is the fourth largest city in the state of New York. If pronounced with the emphasis on the "o" and "n" as in Yooonnnkers, you will sound like a true New Yorker. But what is Yonkers? Growing up there, the thought had never even crossed my mind. It was just a place, a wasteland of our youth.

The city of Yonkers belongs to the legacy of the Hudson Valley area settled by the Dutch explorers. In the 1600's a certain Andrian Van der Donck owned most, if not all, of the surrounding lands north of New York City and the Bronx border. He must have been quite the hustler. He had a reputation as a lady's man. Folks called him Jonkheer and any "gentleman" who had a way about him with women was referred to as a Jonker. The name stuck, and the city became known as Yonkers.

The area eventually grew from rural farms into a haven for manufacturing. The industrial jobs brought in new immigrants who moved up from New York City to expand their status and families. By the fifties, Yonkers was a postwar suburb of upwardly mobile ethnic groups. This suburban dream had the convenience of an easy commute, by bus or subway, into higher paying jobs in the city. Dads were home in time for dinner while moms handled the kids. Neighborhoods were carved out of extended families of similar backgrounds. Being in such proximity to New York City, Yonkers had little in the way of culture or entertainment to offer. Whatever social activity emerged reflected the orientation and territory of its particular communities - the Italian Social Club, the Irish Community Center, the Jewish Center, Saint Rocco Polish Society and the Puerto Rican Nationals. All these groups had conservative values and left little to attract or amuse the generation who would become known as "boomers". We were restless for something else in life.

Yonkers offered us no local heroes to aspire to. For us it was a place with a funny name where we hung out and wasted time. Turns out Yonkers did have its share of talented and creative people, but growing up, we never heard of them. Not until years later would celebrities admit they called Yonkers their hometown. It has been said that Ella Fitzgerald could be heard singing from the tiny church on School Street in downtown Yonkers. Among other well-knowns not known to us were, Gene Krupa the jazz drummer, actor Jon Voight brother to "Wild Thing" singer songwriter Chip Taylor and father to Angelina Jolie, Your Show of Shows fame Sid Caesar, Yonkers' most darling daughter Linda Lovelace and then there's the question of Lady Gaga. A quote from the Bronxville Tribune, January 14, 2010 reads. "Gaga says she's not from Yonkers. So stop spreading those nasty rumors. Lady Gaga reveals to Jay Leno that the worst rumor she's heard about herself is that she's from Yonkers. 'I Love the Bronx but I'm not from Yonkers. There's all sorts of rumors about ne but that's my least favorite' she said." Oh well, sorry Yonkers not Gaga.

Yonkers' biggest contribution to our lives was the Cross-County Shopping Center. Built in the fifties, it was the suburban housewife's dream. A mecca of the many products and household items advertised, tempting all with the desired lifestyle as seen on TV. But there was a price. Our mothers spent countless hours fixated there - like the zombies of Max Brookes' novel, WWZ, they marched forth to the Cross-County Shopping Center.

They were their own version of the 'living dead" with nothing better to do with themselves but shop.

Gimbles Department Store 1950's at Cross County Shopping Center, Yonkers

Part 1

Everyone steals something at some time or another.
You steal a kiss, you steal time, you steal a heart.
There is no moral question, there is only necessity for the object stolen.
Steal this book, 1971 Abby Hoffman.
Steal a few minutes of your time.
Steal my sunshine.
Steal a little piece of my heart.
Steal third base, then steal home.

Chapter 1
Groundhog Day, 1970

Ok, so what happened between the ages of 15 and 19? That is only four years in a person's life. Within those four years, I lost my virginity, started art school, got my nose broken then fixed, hitchhiked to school for a year, masterminded a bank heist and pulled it off.

I went from wallflower to wildflower.

Virginity first. My steady boyfriend was a product of a single parent home. Today that does not really get a response, but back then there was a bad stigma attached to it. I grew up in Yonkers, just a few miles north of New York City. I came from a family of good Italian Catholics. My parents were miserable, but in the decades immediately following WWII, good Catholic parents stayed together regardless of how much they fought and argued. They stayed together, no matter how much they resented each other. They stayed together because the church did not allow divorce.

My boyfriend Patrick - nicknamed 'Doc' - supplied everyone with drugs. His single parent mom was busy raising four kids and working nine to five as a teller in a bank. She could have cared less about what went on in her house while she was at work. By the time she got home, she was usually toasted. Mrs. McBride was short, fair-skinned, rosy- cheeked, and very Irish. Her kids were Cathleen, Patrick, Bernadette and 'Danny Boy', the youngest. Her boyfriend was from Malta and had a dominant mustache that rivaled Dali's. It dominated his face, just like Dali's curlicued trademark, except it was much fatter. He spoke with a thick accent and wore a gold Maltese cross around his neck.

We cut school a lot, and Doc's place was the safe place to be. Our core gang of hookies included myself and Doc, my cousin Mike and his girlfriend Sue, Charlie and his girlfriend Martina. We were the regulars who often welcomed drop-in friends. Our day was simple; we got laid and we got high.

I used to watch my friends as they tightened rubber bands till a vein swelled. Someone would rant on about how bad the Grateful Dead were. They are dead. Kill. Tap the needle. Push and release slowly. My good friend Charlie had the look of the Mad Hatter, but when this stuff hit his veins his eyes rolled back, and he seemed angelic. His girlfriend, Martina, always talked in a soft sing song voice. She appeared to not touch the ground when she walked either. I was lucky. I hated needles. I never did junk.

Charlie and Martina, Doc and I, hung out a lot together. It was a funny thing. Charlie and I were close friends, but we were never a couple. We were both olive-skinned Italian American kids with similar families. Martina and Doc, on the other hand, were Irish. They both had blue eyes, fair skin, and alcoholic parents. They were not friends. After all the teenage sex had exhausted these relationships, only Charlie and I would remain friends.

Our gang did a lot of aimless driving around at night. There was nothing to do but hang around with whoever happened to have a car. Sometimes we would meet up with other kids in other cars just cruising around. We were gypsies, as Pete Townsend said, "Air-conditioned gypsies, going mobile." Usually stoned, music blaring, we would drive between The Bronx and Yonkers border, the reservoir, and Gun Hill Road, with Cross-County Center, a huge outdoor shopping mall, as the vortex.

Sometimes you hear a song, and you know exactly where you were and what you were doing when you first heard it. The memory of how you felt at that moment never leaves you.

I first met Charlie while a couple of us were driving around one night. We had stopped at the gas station along the Thruway on the edge of the Cross-County Center. My cousin's cousin on his father's side worked graveyard shift at the gas station. This kid was green, 'just off the boat' from Italy. Everyone I knew was second generation, but this kid was a fresh arrival. His English was questionable, but he understood more than most people realized, conveniently, of course, when it was necessary to engage with the teachers at Lincoln High School which we all attended. He looked foreign with his wild hair, the way he dressed, his fast gestures - like dance movements - and he was always grinning.

That night everyone could not stop talking about how crazy my cousin's cousin was. He had robbed the gas station where he worked, bragging about how much money was in the register. He told the police and his boss that the thieves drove in from the Thruway and drove off again, heading north with the money. Maybe it was his dumb English, dumb luck, or immigrant charm, but the police believed him. Everyone talked about it. What a crazy dude. Only a greaser straight from Italy would try something like that. Maybe everyone in Italy did things like rob their place of employment. Everyone laughed because the cops were not interested in small change robberies. They were either going after drug dealers or dealing themselves. Everyone thought it even crazier that my cousin's cousin was still working at the gas station. Sick pup.

While parked at the gas station, Charlie and a girl he was with, started making out in the back seat, unaware, or at least appearing unaware, of those already wedged in beside them. It was an ordinary night with cars on the Thruway steadily speeding past. The station smelled of gas, oil, and beer. Huge billboards surrounded us that defined our existence. There were massive Lichtenstein heads shouting to us in it's huge red letters drink a Coca Cola or smoke Camel cigarettes. Billboards were stacked one right after the other, a veritable pop-art army of advertisements.

Surrounded by billboards, along with neon lights, and car lights, someone in the front seat messed with the radio. They were switching the dials from station to station, trying to find something worth listening to. Suddenly, they stopped, having found what they were searching for.

The song streamed out of the dashboard. "It's a little bit funny, this feeling inside…."

I remember thinking, how beautiful the song was. I thought, 'This is what I want. I want someone, someday to love me the way Elton John loves the person he is addressing in Your Song. "How wonderful life is while you're in the world." Not too much to ask.

Charlie was my age and in many of my classes. He was part of our crowd. He played lead guitar in his own band. They called themselves Sapphire. I designed their t-shirts, the lettering for the name Saphire was a thin lean font with a large dominating S creating the appearance of being a lightning bolt and of course I choose a deep ultramarine blue for the color. Charlie and I connected intellectually, and for a while, Charlie was the background of my life.

In 1972, Charlie and I had been the first kids in our high school to register to vote. It was Nixon's token gesture to the hippie generation. Since he was sending the males of our generation off to war, he must have thought he might as well let them vote. Maybe that would shut the kids up. Charlie and I hopped on a bus in March right after my 18th birthday and registered to vote. We were going to be part of changing the world. We talked about life and death and our someday children and our parents and all society's materialistic demons and how good Stevie Wonder sounded.

Despite his easy-going nature, Charlie had a darkness to him. There was always something pulling at his soul. Years later at his funeral, his father said he was a tormented soul. But at the time, I was looking only at his light, believing the best would come. I have since learned that we all possess a darkness. The trick is learning how to see in the dark.

As my sixteenth birthday approached, I decided I did not want to be 'sweet' sixteen. Sweet sixteen and dating all seemed to belong to a distant and different era, somewhere in the fifties. Sweet sixteen conjured up images of that syrupy girl in the Sound of Music, all saccharine and smiles. Life was not that way, and I suspected love was not either. I figured if I was going to go all the way with sex thing, it should be celebrated. At first Doc and I just did the heavy teenage petting thing. Inevitably, in addition to the drugs at Doc's

ome, the kids cutting school got into sex. It became our other
ntertainment of choice. Teenage sex being what it is, inexperienced
hyper-hormone kids trying to be cool, was also pretty unmemorable.
What I did remember was the date, February 2. I lost my virginity at
Doc's house, cutting school with a bunch of other kids, getting high
on Groundhog Day. I like to think that day the groundhog saw his
shadow, but I do not recall.

Charlie 1972

Chapter 2
Tinkerbell

I first met Doc at my cousin Michael's house. They were close friends. My aunt would pay me to come over to clean her house. I hated polishing silverware, but I think teaching me the value of cleaning silverware was my mother's idea of training me to be a good housewife. Anyway, I would also answer the door like the hired help my aunt treated me as. One day, Doc was at the door to see my cousin. I never talked to Doc at my cousin's house. I was too shy! The first time I spoke to him was in that one place where most teenage romances start, detention. We recognized each other when he was sitting behind me.

Doc and my cousin Mike were a year older than me. The other kids would tease Doc saying, "You couldn't date Mike, so you started dating his cousin." It was fun because I was close to my cousin.

Mike had a great imagination. He was in a band, they called themselves Hi Blues Condition. My sister, who is a year younger than me, was dating the bass player in the band. We would go to all the concerts together. We were part of the 'in' crowd.

Doc supplied drugs and his drug of choice was acid. His use of it grew, as his reputation for carrying the best acid around grew. Acid would often make him paranoid, and I took note of how his paranoia was manifesting itself into more and more frequent and violent outbursts. At first, I witnessed him kicking his dog, then, stoned out of his mind, he kicked his kid brother down the stairs. It was not good. I had a feeling that one day I might be in Doc's kid brother's place. When I finally did fall victim, it was the power of a film which provided the spark that unleashed his wrath.

Doc was tripping when we went to see A Clockwork Orange. The best thing about living in Yonkers, or perhaps the only good thing about Yonkers, was the simple fact that you could catch a bus to anywhere. The buses ran every fifteen minutes from and to anywhere. Downtown Manhattan, Getty Square, Cross-County Center, White Plains. It appeared as though all desired destinations were only fifteen minutes from anywhere in Yonkers.

I was waiting for a bus. I was wearing a pair of dark sunglasses and hoping that nobody would see me. There is logic that says if you're behind dark sunglasses no one will see you, or at least they won't recognize you if they do. But this is not true. In fact, Charlie pulled up in his car with his friend Skip (aka Steve) and said, "Get in Mare, I'll give you a ride."

I did not say anything. I just got in. Honestly, I really wanted someone to recognize me because I did not recognize myself. I slid into the back of Charlie's old rusty car. He and Skip had become a hangout team since Charlie's girlfriend, Martina, left him. Skip looked a lot like Jerry Garcia, something he was not thrilled about since he was not a fan of The Dead. He would go off on long rants about how awful they were. Skip was another Italian kid from a messed-up family. If someone made the unfortunate remark of how much he looked like Garcia, the result was both sad and comical, bordering on insanity. The worst part is that Skip did have a keen music sensibility, and he aspired to be a DJ. He had managed, after many concerts, to get close to bands, even getting invited onto tour buses to party. We could not figure out how he squirreled his way in. Maybe they thought he was Garcia, too.

Charlie stared at me through the rearview mirror and said, "Take off the glasses." I hesitated, but finally did. "Fuckin' Doc!" Charlie was pissed. "He did this to you, didn't he! Fuckin' Doc!" Charlie drove me to the hospital.

Both of my eyes were black, and my nose was cracked in the middle. I looked like a prizefighter who had just lost 14 rounds. I sat in the back of that car crying. I cried because someone cared about what had happened to me.

Earlier that day, at my parent's house, it was a different story. I do not remember getting into bed or falling asleep the night before, but I do remember how my family reacted when I stumbled out of bed and into the kitchen in the morning. Nobody seemed to care, or at least they did not act like they did. It was Saturday so everyone was home eating breakfast. I remember the look on their faces, my mother, my father, my brothers, and my sister. It was something between horror and fear. My beat-up face just confirmed to them that I was 'trouble.' Maybe my parents did not physically hurt me over the years, but they certainly did hurt me emotionally. Suddenly, this physical manifestation seemed logical. I told my parents that the car door hit me. They did not question it. They wanted to believe me.

My nose got fixed. The doctor who performed the surgery accepted a painting of mine in return for the work. Charlie and Skip came to see me in the hospital. The only problem with that was they made me laugh. Bandages were wrapped around my face and nose like a horror film mummy. Laughing is hard to do after that kind of surgery, but it was the only thing that got me through the whole mess. Crazy thing is, laughing was why Doc hit me. I was laughing at him. We were at Doc's house when he asked his mom if he could borrow the car. She told him sure but first he had to move the boards that were piled up in the front yard into the back like she had asked him to do all week and he didn't get around to it. Simple enough. They were large, eighteen foot long two by fours. Doc was carrying them one at a tine balancing them on his head and holding onto them with his hands on both sides, as a result both ends of the boards bounced along the way. Watching him I was reminded of an episode of Laurel and Hardy that was hilarious. I started laughing. Next thing I know, Doc is red-faced and pissed and says, "What the hell you laughing at." Wham! He was stoned on acid and, paranoia being what it is, my laughter made him mad, and rage took over. He whacked me in the face while we were parked in his car outside his house. Maybe it was too many drugs. Thing is, I knew it would happen, eventually. It was only a matter of time. Blood ran out of my nose like a faucet turned on full. Suddenly I felt like I was in a Looney Tunes cartoon with stars spinning around my head. Doc's mom came running out of the house and had me tilt my head back to stop the bleeding. She handed me an ice pack, and when the bleeding stopped, Doc drove me home.

I was admitted to Professional Hospital in Yonkers and heard stories on the news while I was there about a fellow patient that my doctor was treating. He was doing plastic surgery on someone who was changing their sex. It was 1974. I could not believe that such a change was possible. I looked around the hospital, and sure enough, down a pretty-well secluded hall, I found the person going through the sex change. They were bandaged a lot. I can still see the look when our eyes locked. I recognized that look. I had seen it in myself many times in the mirror. Who am I? It seemed I was going through my own kind of change.

My parents, in a final act of disgust with who I was becoming, packed my books and put them at the foot of my bed. In fact, they packed all my stuff. I finally got the message. I did not belong there.

At the time, I was commuting up to Rockland Community College as an Art Major. My parents, refused to pay a nickel towards my tuition unless I went to school for nursing. That made sense to them. Did they truly see me as a nurse? Not really. Their actual motive was obvious. They had a friend whose daughters went to nursing school, and those girls were dating doctors. My parents wanted me to follow the same path. They wanted me to become a nurse, date, and then marry a doctor. But I had other ideas.

I put myself through art school by working two jobs - one at Gimbels, the big department store that competed with Macy's, and the other as a student assistant to Edgar Levy, an Art History Instructor at RCC. I had my jobs. I had school. I was ready to leave home.

I moved in with Joann, a girl from high school. She was studying to be a hairdresser. Charlie had nicknamed her "the sultan's favorite." Joann was a well-rounded Puerto Rican and had the biggest boobs in the world. On several occasions, her boobs saved us all from getting busted. If we saw the cops trailing us, everyone would put their joints out and pass them to Joann. She would lift those wondrous mamas and tuck everything under her boobs. The sultan's favorite. We even decorated her room like a harem with drapes, big pillows, a pipe, and pictures of Mick Jagger everywhere.

Decades later, Charlie and I went to see Joann. By then, I had a sixteen-year-old in tow. Joann had brought the house right next door to the one where we had our first apartment. She described it on the phone "Remember that bitch who used to call the cops on us all the time? I brought her house when she died." That is justice for you. It was fully furnished.

But I am jumping ahead.

The summer of '74, the kids I hung out with all wanted to get tattoos. A tattoo became a symbol of who we were. Some of us were seniors. We knew we would be going into the unknown dark space, not quite in the adult world, not still children - a place never to be seen again. The restlessness of summer germinated into nights hanging out at the playground. Being in the playground at night was like being in limbo; it existed between two worlds. We needed a souvenir, a tribal mark, a ritual designed to initiate the members, brand us, and mark our passage into the wider world, when summer was over.

It was illegal in Yonkers to get a tattoo, but that was not going to stop us. Everyone was asking me to draw something customized for his or her tats. Joann got a pair of scissors on her shoulder; Mike got Beatles notes; and Bobby got a Surreal-looking figure. As for finding a place to get our tats, Mike knew a guy over the city border in Mount Vernon. It was under the subway line. Everyone from the playground went there, using the sketch I had drawn, for their tattoo. Finally, it was my turn. I hated needles. I still hate needles. I almost passed out as this guy came at me with his gigantic tattoo needle. "So, you're my competition. You get yours for free." I choose to have my tat on my ass. Actually, it was on my right upper thigh, totally visible when I was wearing a bathing suit. It did not really hurt much through the fat. My tattoo was Tinkerbell.

drawing of Joann as the "Sultan's favorite"

Chapter 3
Roaming the Perimeter

The apartment with Joann was pretty much what you could expect based on what two eighteen-year-old girls could afford- small and cheap. It was a basement apartment in a modest row house located in the central eastern corridor of Yonkers, an area where houses were stacked close together, bordering the Bronx. The neighborhood was developed in the fifties and consisted of Irish, Italian, and Jewish middleclass families. We were within walking distance to the Bronx River Parkway just two blocks east. The Bronx was on the other side of the highway.

There was just enough space between houses to have a walkway on one side leading to our basement apartment. Out back was a sitting area. The area was also accessible by stairs from the main living quarters. We never used the outside sitting area since it was exclusively for the landlord. The yard to our house was fenced in like most of the other yards. The only difference between our fence and those enclosing the other yards, was that the fence at our place was an industrial fence; it was also slightly higher than the other fences. Along with the heavy-duty fence, the landlord had two huge guard dogs that patrolled the property. The combined effect of the high fence and the guard dogs was the sense of being in a fortress. The dogs stood three feet tall on all four legs and had constant drool streaming from their mouths. When they barked, you knew to keep a safe distance from them. The dogs were trained to attack anyone not associated with our landlord. We had to be introduced to the dogs before moving in, to familiarize them with us. Most of the time the pair roamed the parameter of the property. But in the evenings, they were brought inside. Joann and I could hear their movements through the ceiling. They were so huge, we always knew just where they were inside, by the sound of their heavy paws on the wooden floors above.

Steve, our landlord, was also Joann's boss. He owned a hair salon on Central Avenue in northern Yonkers. It was a lucrative business in a huge high-rise apartment complex with a loyal customer base. Joann and I kept our place quiet, and although we were the first and only kids our age to get our own apartment, we kept visitors to a minimum. Limited traffic in and out of our apartment was a request of the landlord; and, as we wanted to stay on good terms, we saw no reason not to abide by his conditions. Besides, none of our friends wanted to deal with the dogs.

Steve was a good ten years older than us, an Italian American greaser, complete with tight black pants, slick hair, and a cigarette always dangling from his mouth, as though it was permanently attached to his lips. Typical of most guys like Steve, he had married his high school sweetheart. At the time, they did not yet have kids. His side business, his real moneymaker, and the reason for all the security, was dealing drugs. He dealt mostly in pills and cocaine. Pot was a lightweight product he carried, almost as an afterthought. Our house was constantly under random surveillance by drug enforcement, but they could never get anything on him. In an odd way, Joann and I felt very protected under the 'safe' roof Steve provided.

My hours had me out early, quietly slipping through the door, so as not to wake Joann. On weekday mornings, I walked two blocks over to the parkway entrance to hitchhike to school. After school, I would find my way back to Yonkers, to my job at Gimbels department store. I would return to the apartment after work, around 11 p.m. Joann usually rode to work with Steve and partied most nights after work with Tina, her best friend since childhood.

Tina was a year younger than us. She and Joann had been tight a long time - since kindergarten. Tina was a stunningly beautiful red-headed, northern Italian girl. She was fixated on David Bowie and went to all his concerts. She even hung out at the clubs Bowie was known to frequent in the city. She wore platform shoes like Bowie and was proud of her ginger red hair, which gave her further passage into Bowie land.

Her beauty was matched only by her dizziness. I was at her house once when she opened a dresser drawer full of neatly folded clothing in her bedroom. "Look, the labels are all still on them. My mom steals them and then has me return them for the cash. Some she keeps for herself."

Tina's mom had been stealing clothes from Gimbels for years. Security did not have a clue. This fifty-year-old, middle-class woman made extra cash stealing stuff from the department store. Tina and her mother did not need the extra money. It was just a pastime for her mom, a sport. Maybe she was bored being just a housewife in Yonkers. Or maybe it was a distraction from the deeper secret in their house.

Some days I would come home from school directly, work on my assignments and crash. I hardly ever heard Joann tiptoeing in after midnight. Joann had the bedroom, and I slept on a daybed in our sitting room. The sitting room was also the entry room and our only other full room. A small kitchenette and bathroom were off the entry room. All in all, the place was perfect.

The routine of our life was efficient and simple, but on a night when I had come home early and fell asleep, while Joann was still out who-knows-where, my sense of safety was shattered. At first, I thought I was having a nightmare, a bad dream. In a deep sleep, I could feel something pressing on my throat. My awareness woke me. I felt the weight of a man on top of me, his hands firmly around my neck, pressing ever harder. I became aware that I could not breathe. I recognized him. It was Tina's older brother and one of Steve's pals. I was tiny under the bulk of his frame and could not budge. I was gasping for air, unable to breathe, unable to move. With a firm grip on my neck, his eyes focused directly into my eyes. He said, "If you ever tell anyone, I'll come back and finish the job." In an instant, I thought I would die. Then he was done, he released his grip, rolled off me, zipped up his pants and left through the door. It happened so fast, yet while he was doing what he did to me, time seemed to move in slow motion.

My brain went immediately into survival mode. I do not have any recollection of how I got into the shower, but I managed, somehow. I stood in the shower crying with water streaming over me. I have no idea when Joann came home, but she found me, still in the shower, sobbing. We had all heard rumors that Tina's two older brothers, had been sexually molesting her since she was a kid, but back then, nobody talked openly about that kind of incestual molestation.

At some point, Joann concluded that the dogs would not have

barked at my assailant, since he had a familiar scent. He had dated the girl who had previously lived in our apartment, and he must have retained a key. The ex-girlfriend was a jockey at Yonkers Raceway and was a huge cokehead. What was even scarier was that he often visited Steve upstairs. That way he must have come to know our movements, our comings and goings. My instincts set this entire episode into the darkest, furthest recesses of my brain. Forget for survival.

It would be a good twenty years before the memory of the event surfaced. It was during a therapy session, following notice of Tina's brother's death. He was done in by the mob for stealing from them. During all the time that lapsed between the rape and the therapy session, I had never told a soul. Neither had Joann.

Chapter 4
Lead Free

I did not see any point in getting a license to drive while living in Yonkers. It was rough enough hustling up tuition and rent. How could I possibly afford a car, insurance, and gas for the damn thing? Besides, I could take buses everywhere. The bus stopped right outside our door. I could crisscross Yonkers to the Bronx, get on the Grand Concourse and be in downtown Manhattan in no time. I could also head north to White Plains, or east to the river. I could take a bus anywhere. Anywhere except across the Hudson River. While living with Joann, I was going to Rockland Community College (RCC), across the Tappan Zee Bridge, in Rockland County. In other words, across the river.

The art program at RCC had an exceptional reputation, as did the music department. Rockland Community College was in Suffern, New York. The commute from Yonkers became a journey, a quest, a fixed destination. I was going against the grain of my family's belief in me. I was supposed to become a nurse, marry a doctor, and have lots of kids. Daughters who were Italian American, first generation, born here, did not go to college. They did not waste money on further schooling after high school, unless the results were practical. Training in fine art was not practical. Only rich kids had that luxury. I was going to prove to my family, to me, to my future self that I could get a degree in the field I wished to pursue. I would do it anyway I could. And I would pay for it myself.

Initially, I got to school with a group from Lincoln High who were carpooling. The carpooling trips to RCC were ridiculous. Silly. Mostly we smoked pot on the way and got lost in our thoughts and the music on the radio. The gas crisis had necessitated carpooling. That year, because of the gas shortage, people were forced to ration. Odd or even. People got gas for their car depending on the last number of their license plate. Was it odd or was it even? It did not seem to matter because the lines for gas were long regardless of what stinking number was on a license plate. It seemed every day was odd. We were all odd in this very uneven world.

The bridge became the connector. The rides from Yonkers to Suffern were a swirl of fragmented conversations and experiences. I want to thank all the people who helped me to cross over the bridge.

Our Lincoln High group decided we should go together. Carpooling would be the solution. We had worked out a schedule. We worked out who paid what to whomever was driving. When Charlie drove, which worked out to be three times a week, every other week, we were always late. He and Skip, who rode shotgun with Charlie, seemed to be in a state of perpetual madness. Yes, even first thing in the morning. It got worse as more odd souls entered the car. Skip selected the music on the days we carpooled in Charlie's car. Pink Floyd. The Doobie Brothers. Aretha. Stevie Wonder. And of course, the Who. We were linked by our need to get from here to there. I was along for the ride. Pat, another kid from high school drove when Charlie was not driving.

When Pat drove, it was a sure thing we would get to RCC on time and in one piece. Floyd rode shotgun when Pat drove. Floyd was a tall, lanky kid from the neighborhood. A girl named Cathy squeezed in between him and Pat. The rest of us piled in the back - me, Charlie, Skip and Doc. We were going to college! Each of us got picked up at our homes. The last stop was Charlie's house at 7:00 am. His mother always yelled after him. She never stopped. Every time we pulled up, she was yelling, broadcasting to anyone in earshot how stupid she thought her son was. When he finally got in the car, his first concern was to get stoned with Skip. Pat compromised and let them have control of the radio instead. This was a relief because Floyd wanted to listen to Neil Diamond, which sent Skip off the deep end. The only thing that put Skip over the edge more than "Sweet Caroline" was Jerry Garcia and the Grateful Dead. Bite them. Bite. It took Pat several weeks to figure out a solution to who's favorite music we would be listening to each day and only after some painful protesting from the back seat did we all agree on "YES" group instead of Neil Diamond or the "Grateful Dead". Heading home, the train always passed under the bridge on the Westchester side, we were going south, the train north. Three cars on a train at three o'clock every Monday with Pat driving. Same schedule every week.

It did not take long, maybe a semester or two, before we started thinning out. Someone would miss a couple of classes here, a week or two there. A month. Gone. Semester over. I kept going to class along with working evenings and weekends at Gimbels department store in the Cross-County Center. In my interview with Gimbels I mentioned I was an Art Major. That bit of info got me placed in the Gift-Wrapping department. "She's an artsy type."

Putting myself through school in addition to sharing Joann's apartment expenses, I needed to work two jobs. The second was during the day at RCC in between classes as student assistant to Edgar Levy. Edgar was the elder of the RCC Art faculty. He was wonderfully enthusiastic, in his late sixties, dapper and a total intellectual snob. His wife, Lucille, had recently passed. I never met her, but I understood she had been a prominent illustrator.

Edgar took to me, which was rare since he did not take to a lot of students. He was an Adjunct Professor and taught Drawing and Art History. I was not in any of his classes, he just noticed me hanging around the department and offered me the job. As his assistant, I essentially got paid to put away the Art History slides that were used for his lectures. Edgar would rush in after his talks and dump the entire lot of slides from the morning Art History class into a basket. My job was to go through them all and file them away. There was a wall of short custom-built shelving for them. Each shelf was labeled with dates, countries and styles. I looked at a lot of slides and got to know and identify where and when each belonged. This, by the way, is probably the best way to learn Art History.

It was during my second year at RCC that I found myself hitch-hiking to get to school. The days of carpooling were over. Yonkers to Rockland, over the bridge. There probably was a simpler way, but the route I chose was interesting, and, besides, what else did I have to do. In the mornings, I would walk from my apartment to the Bronx River Parkway.

Just like as the name implies, there was a river beside the parkway, and I always stopped to spit into it when I crossed it. It was something Charlie and I used to do. Every time we crossed a bridge over water, we spit into it. Why? To add our life, a part of ourselves to the water and watch it cross under on its way to somewhere else. In our minds, we believed we could be somewhere else, too. Out of here. Out of Yonkers. Out of the frustration of being in-between. At least, some essence of us dreamed of being elsewhere.

After my ritual spit, I would start hitchhiking. The parkway would take me north to the Sprain Brook Parkway or New York State Thruway. Whichever way anyone was going was fine with me. I just needed to get over the bridge.

People who pick up hitchhikers are interesting, as interesting as the hitchhikers they pick up, and I was no exception. I do believe that I got rides quickly and easily because my hair had blue stripes in it. I imagined my head must have looked like a BRILLO Pad to the drivers who picked me up. Just like in advertising, color sells, and blue was working just fine for me.

I started to keep a journal of those rides. It was an old standard blank book ledger from my grandfather's shoe repair store that I rescued from the cellar at my parent's house. I wrote down a sentence or two, or a drawing or maybe just a quote from the day's ride. Using my design skills, I created a logo and called it "Lead Free".

Some days it rained, some days it snowed. When the sky was blue, I could feel the brilliant sun. But every day as I stuck my thumb out to the road, I was standing alone. Hitchhiking gave me a lot of time by myself spent on entrance ramps and side roads in all kinds of weather. All that alone time became times I had to think. Think about where I was going, think about how I was getting there. Thumb out, my dreams intact.

Every day I met someone new and everyone became my friend during the time I spent in their car, crossing the bridge. Here are some excerpts from my journal of some of those rides:

● "Mike, what is reality?" Mike just looked up and said, "What is reality? Anybody ever tell you you're a crazy Italian. Where do you come from?"

Where am I going?

● A businessman wanted to "make it" so I gave him a phony name and address. Hope he goes there.

● Old man from Monroe stopped at a bakery and brought me a gingerbread cookie when he found out it was my birthday. I asked him where he was going. He said he was following the rainbow. I asked if I could come, he said no.

He was a preacher.

● A couple had coke paraphernalia all over the car and I could tell they were stoned. Two little girls sat in the back seat with me. The girls started to talk about the lady who jumped off the bridge. The kids were saying to each other, "Pool, let's go over the pool. Are we going inside that bridge?" Jazz music played on.

● A displaced Vietnam vet tells me he has no home. His parents sold his childhood home in Queens and moved up to Rockland while he was on duty in Nam. He's lost. He tells me we should spend the day together as he slides a pistol from his jacket. I don't react to it and tell him that's a good idea. I ask why don't we stop at a diner and get some breakfast first. I know a good one in Nyack, it's just off the highway. My instincts serve me well. I stay calm as we sit down in the diner. I order and tell him I need to use the lady's room. He's smiling and looking over the menu, today he has a purpose and company. I grab my bag that contains all my stuff, head to the back of the diner and slide out the back door. I know the back streets of Nyack and run, darting through traffic. I feel bad for this displaced vet.

● Standing just past the Ardsley Exit, a State Trooper pulls up to me. He gets out and asks my name and where I'm going. I tell him I'm an art student at RCC in Rockland County. I pull out a class project from my bag to prove it. I tell him it's the only way I can get to school. He orders me into the police car. I'm thinking my day is screwed, I'm never getting to school today. He orders me to buckle my seat belt. He then proceeds to do ninety miles an hour up the Thruway over the bridge and drives me right to the art building at RCC. "Don't let me catch you out there on the road like that again. OK. Be careful.

Steve working inside the radio station at Rockland Community College 1973

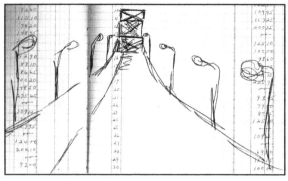

sketches from my journal LeadFree drawn while hitch-hiking from Yonkers
to Rockland Community College 1973

Chapter 5
In Plain Sight

Summer months in hangout land meant time spent in parking lots
just hanging around. Get out of work and meet up in a parking lot.
Everyone would be there sitting on a concrete curb in a parking
lot after work. The bumpers were chipped from too many car lips
smacking up against them. Staring at grease stained rainbows and
orbs of black gum that dotted the asphalt was how summer nights
were spent. We were in an alternative universe. It felt two-dimension-
al, like we were cut-outs moving or sliding through space.

Charlie and I developed a confidence. Sitting with Charlie on the
concrete curb we exchanged our inner secrets, dreams, and details
of our mundane lives. Our jobs were lame. Getting a paycheck was
lame, and just getting by was even lamer. There had to be a better
way. Dealing drugs was one way. Charlie usually ate up his profits.

On a not so special night, drinking beer in a parking lot, surrounded by the urban rodeo chaos of hanger-outers, I finally said it out
loud to Charlie. It was finally out of my brain, something I had been

thinking about for months. I finally said "Charlie, there's got to be a way to get our hands on all that money! You know, the money..."

Gift Wrapping at Gimbels department store was kind of fun. Customers would line up six or more deep on any given holiday to have our small team of talented gift wrappers embellish their items. Who would pay to have someone else wrap their gifts? The men. Especially the men who brought wives and girlfriends beautiful things for Valentine's Day or birthdays or Christmas. Or the fathers on Mother's Day, or the mother's with kids on Father's Day. Then there were the shoppers with money and no time to wrap gifts. People who would tell us they were all thumbs and could never do what we did. A lot of shoppers wanted gifts wrapped, and some of them tipped us, too. It was an easy job. I was the youngest of the group of women who worked in the department. They seemed so much older than me and appeared to have been in the department for decades. I was the novelty, so young and so energetic, always smiling, with blue hair highlights and cute boyfriends, who occasionally picked me up after work.

We stood behind a long counter stocked with ribbons and accessories to go with every special gift giving occasion: little baby shoes in pink and blue or rattles to adorn the top of a baby shower gift; wedding rings for the bride-to-be package; clown motifs for kid events; all kinds of trinkets for that moment in life where a gift is added to the celebration. And to make it easy, a sample poster was on display for customers to choose from. The accessories were in the drawers under the counter. Behind us were rolls and rolls of wrapping paper. There were paper designs for every possible occasion. This included the newly formed Afro-American print in black, green, and red named for the newly created Afro-American holiday Kwanzaa.

It was a busy job when we were busy and a slow, boring, clock-ticking job when we were not. Gift Wrapping was on the third floor, the top floor of the store, out of the way. It was in an enclosed backroom - almost an afterthought - as we were separated from the rest of the openness of the other departments. In addition to giftwrapping, the small department took exchanges and handed out refunds. It kind of reminded me of what it was like to play store as a kid. A cash box under the counter next to all those cute gift-wrapping accessories.

"Do you have your receipt?" No register, just cash payouts. Our box contained one thousand to five thousand dollars or more around Christmas and New Year's.

"You know that money," I said again to Charlie.

Sitting in front of me every night at Gimbels was this cash. It seemed a simple solution, a simple outrageous solution to our urgent desires to 'get outta there'

My financial situation was desperate, and the desperation drove my imagination. I was struggling. I was working two jobs and paying rent with no idea as to how I was going to afford another semester at RCC. I had filled out all the financial aid forms I could and continued to be rejected. What the heck! How poor did you need to be to qualify for New York State financial aid? I did not want to take out a student loan. A lot of kids did that only to drop out and find themselves in debt.

I was so desperate I decided to visit my Mom, to beg her for help. It was beyond humiliating, but I called her and arranged to stop in for lunch. When I arrived, she was her usual critical, ice queen self. Minor pleasantries were exchanged and then she asked, "Are you dating anyone?" My response, "No Mom, that's not what I do at

chool." "Well," she says, "what do you want?" as she put together a
una fish sandwich then cut it in half. I did not hesitate to tell her. "I
ould really use some money toward tuition. I'm short a few hundred
ollars."

She passed me the sandwich and did not say a word. I did not think
ny request was outrageous, especially since each of my brothers
vere given five hundred dollars when they graduated high school,
o get them started in life. Neither of them even attempted to go to
ollege. My sister and I were never given a cent, nothing. I needed
unds then and there.

Mom just walked over to her cash jar, which sat in the dining room
on a shelf with the dishes. She pulled out a roll of bills and placed a
wenty on the table next to the dish with the tuna fish sandwich. "I
xpect you to pay me back."

I was hungry, said nothing, took a couple of bites from my sand-
vich then picked up the twenty and left. Shutting the door behind
ne, I felt guilty and ashamed for asking. Then I got angry.

It was not until four years later, during my final semester, that
discovered why I had been refused financial aid. A kindhearted
ecretary took pity on me and said she would make some calls on my
ehalf. A few weeks later she informed me, "Your parents have been
laiming you as a dependent and according to the guidelines this
lisqualifies you for assistance. Sorry hon."

Not only did my parents not give me any help, but they were also
naking money on me as a deduction on their taxes, and I was paying
he price.

A boring, long, and hot summer rolled over into fall, and every
other evening I delivered another scenario to Charlie. I would go on
nd on with another fantastic plot about extracting the cash from

Gimbels Gift Wrapping department without getting caught. Most nights Charlie was annoyed at my naiveté. He would quickly pick each plot apart. He pointed out the flaws and the ridiculousness, "That is way too complicated," or "What are you watching? The cops would be on to you. You can't get tied up. How does that make any sense?"

As an avid drug user, Charlie had been avoiding the law for years and had a lot more experience in identifying inaccurate and inconsistent propositions. He reminded me of a mouse who knows exactly where and when the cat is sleeping and how to sneak past him without getting caught. Some nights he would just shake his head no.

"I saw Martina today; she had a baby." Charlie was bummed by the news about his high school girlfriend. He trailed off. His eyes were fixed on something far away. He did not seem to really hear anything else I said that night sitting on a concrete curb in a parking lot. Or so I thought.

"You know, the best way to get the money out of the store is the simplest way." Charlie turned to listen, his eyes gazing at me. "I simply wrap it up in a gift box. You know with nice birthday paper, ribbons, an accessory on top, make it look nice and special and you come in and carry it out. No one knows there's money inside it except you and me." Charlie turned his head towards me. He smiled. I am elated at his response. It requires us to be partners. "You will walk out into the night right under their noses and drive away with the money. We'll split it fifty-fifty later."

Charlie tested me with a barrage of questions. What was the security like? When was closing time? Did I work alone? Could I handle a lie detector test?

Then he said, "We shouldn't have any contact with each other for a week, two maybe, even three afterwards. NONE. There needs to be no association, no tracing anybody. That means no calls, nothing."

I smiled at him. "I trust you. You trust me to deal with Security?"

"I don't know Mare, that's tricky"

I let him know. "Charlie, I think I figured that out. If it's done when Security is busy doing something else, it should be a breeze. Security in that place is a joke."

Chapter 6
Super Bowl Sunday

This jerk in Security kept asking me out. His name was Don. I could go with him to find out more about what Security did and how they did it. Charlie agreed. "Good idea. Get him to show you their offices, where they are, look for cameras, how many guys are working at any given time."

I decided to have lunch with the guy during my break on a Saturday evening. Don was a macho guy, five years older than me. He was everything I despised in a guy: slick hair, an ugly suit that did not fit, black shoes. And he did not stop talking about himself.

We went next door to the restaurant where he had us sit at the bar. The place was dark and slow for a Saturday evening. Don said hello to another security guard, a woman in her forties. She was working on a beer but clearly, from her voice, had already had a few. Her hair was a mess. She was sloppy, elbow up against her chin, a cigarette in one hand. Don said, "We all like this place. They got great food here." I assumed by now that the "we" meant Security, and by the look of the few other people in the restaurant, I was assuming correctly. He ordered a drink with a burger and fries. I did not react to the drink. I asked for a ginger ale and a tuna sandwich.

He lived in his parents' basement and had been working Security at Gimbels for three years. He told me someday he wanted to be a cop. I was counting on that. Before I returned to work, Don offered to give me a tour of the Security offices, which happened to be in the bowels of Gimbels, levels away from my post in Gift Wrapping. "Oh, you have an office?" This just kept getting better, I thought to myself.

"Come on I'll show you. This place is so cheap."

We went down to a floor I did not know existed, into a dark hall. A sign on the door said Security. There were lockers. with names on them, for coats and personal items - a total of five. There was one beige phone hanging on the wall with multiple buttons on it, a card table, folding chairs, cigarette butts spilling over in a dirty ashtray, and a sign on a door that read "Toilet."

There was no multi-paneled alarm system. No cameras seeing anything, anywhere throughout the entire store. There was another guy asleep on an old couch. Don pointed out that the guy worked the graveyard. "What's a graveyard?" I say as if I had no idea, as if I was too inexperienced to understand.

Don then dutifully explained to the cute girl from upstairs Gift Wrapping who he had been trying to get a date with for months. "That's after the store closes. It's not as if the guy actually does anything. Trying to keep from smiling, I told Don, "I gotta get back. Jen will be waiting for me. She leaves her shift for the night when I get back from my break."

"I know what you mean, it's just me and the guy on the couch after ten o'clock."

Oh really, I thought to myself!

Don escorted me up all three escalators to the third floor. He was proud to display me to all the other guys who probably told him he would never get a date with the chick in Gift Wrapping.

"I don't think Security is going to be a problem. The sooner we do this, the better. Super Bowl Sunday is a few days away, one of the biggest party weekends." I filled Charlie in, spelling out the routine Security followed when they closed at night. "We could do this around that time. It'll disorient them, especially if they've been drinking." I'll tell him he can come and take the gift box filled with money about twenty minutes before closing, when Security's preoccupied.

Charlie gave me a not-so-sure-about-this look.

"I tell you what," I went on. "We do this the night before Super Bowl Sunday when Security, just like the rest of the entire country, everywhere, everyone is preoccupied with Super Bowl Sunday. That is the perfect time to do this - the Saturday before the Super Bowl."

You would think nothing else in the world happened that weekend. Everything on TV, the radio, in stores, restaurants, bars, all advertising and all brain thoughts were focused on Super Bowl Sunday. I could not give a damn about football. I knew nothing about it nor did I want to, but I did know everyone was completely absorbed that day on that game. Everyone was obsessed with what they would eat, who they would watch the game with, what team they wanted to win. On and on and on.

To seal the date with Charlie, I mentioned two things. First, if the police wanted to question me, I would take some downers so I could pass a lie detector test. Downers would slow my heart rate and calm me enough to pass. The second thing I mentioned was timing. "I'm supposed to leave two days afterward for London, England."

Chapter 7
My Man

I saved every penny the summer before to afford a trip to London. RCC's art department belonged to a consortium of community coleges that offered travel for credit. I signed up for the ten-day trip to London for two credits of Art History. Edgar Levy, my boss at RCC, had told me about the trip during the previous semester. He thought it would benefit me. I would gain a lot from such a trip. It was not too pricey. Students stayed in hotels that the consortium booked for art students from the tri-state area. That kept the price down.

I would be out of the country and safe. For me, England was the land that welcomed Jimmy Hendrix and made him a star, an international sensation. England was the land of Pink Floyd and crazy Sid Barrett, now sitting in a looney bin, swallowed by his imagination.

Edgar was going as mentor for the RCC students. We had a rigorous schedule of museums to visit, paintings to see and lectures to attend. When we got back home, there would be a paper to write. All this for two credits of Art History.

So, the date was set.

A month earlier I had gone into a Post Office. There on the table against the wall, reserved for putting stamps and addresses on letters and packages, was a small flappable file with pages for 'Most Wanted Criminals.' Black and white photos, names, and descriptions- - 5'10," approximately 225 lbs., last seen in the Bronx. WANTED. Each listing in the exact same format. Front photo. Side photo. A stack of them. Nobody would notice one missing. They were all dusty, as though the file had not been perused in ages.

The next time I went into the Post Office, I addressed a letter close to the file. I was just another customer so nobody really saw me as I slipped one page from the mid-section of someone wanted for robbery. No one would notice it missing. I curled it up in my hand and crimped it into my pocket.

Now I had my man, my thief. After all, he was already "WANTED." I committed him to memory. I would study his profile every day. He would become real as life. I had a visual to confirm what he looked like, an image.

This was my guy. The guy I would say robbed me. The guy who would order me to put the money in a gift box. The guy who would say he had a gun. The guy in the black and white photo that I saw on a visit to the Post Office. It made me wonder. Did anybody ever really get caught from those 5x7 Wanted photos?

Chapter 8
The Unsaid

The moment after Charlie left the Gift-Wrapping Department with his 'gift,' the air became thick, heavier. The room started shrinking. Everything became silent and screaming at the same time. I could hear all the gift wrap, all the ribbon, all the accessories screaming at me, "Are YOU CRAZY? What have you done? What are you thinking?!"

Then something I never thought could happen happened. My hands started to close. My fingers contracted into a lobster claw. Paralyzed, unable to open. All those "Thou Shalt Nots" screamed at me at once. Thou shalt not steal, thou shalt not covet thy neighbor's goods, thou shalt not lie. Breathe. Breathe. I can do this. I can do this. I must do this. There is no going back now!

Slowly my fingers loosened up and unraveled. I forced myself to shove all the Catholic school guilt, the indoctrination, into the back of my mind. Believe in yourself. You have a plan and it is a good plan. Breathe. Remember what is next. You have been robbed! Ring the damn alarm buzzer!

Trembling with feigned terror from a crime I had just committed, I reached under the counter for the red button that would alert Security that Gift Wrapping had just been robbed. No going back. Shaking and sweating with fear, I pressed the red button, over and over. Nothing happened! A light was supposed to go off to signal that Security had been alerted. Maybe I had not hit the buzzer hard enough. Maybe I needed to press it deeper. Nothing. I pressed the alarm button again and again. Nothing. 'Are you kidding? It doesn't work?!!'

I remembered what the Supervisor had said, when I was being trained for the job. . "And if you ever happen to get robbed, press this red button. The red button under the counter here. It will turn on and light up. Perpetrators will not see it or even hear it, but you can feel safe knowing Security has seen it and is on their way. Not that we have ever been robbed here."

I turned without thinking and reached for the phone. Despite my panic, somehow my brain knew to pick up the inter-departmental phone. It would connect me to the beige phone down in Security. Assholes! I dialed Security. "I've been robbed! At gunpoint! I've been robbed! Up here in Gift Wrapping."

Breathe. I was still trembling when a Security Guard finally reached the third floor Gift Wrapping department. As I started to explain the pretend details, I was crying. Crying from nerves and relief. And as might have been expected, the guard reeked of booze.

It was dumb luck that the alert did not work. Later, Security would get a whipping for having an inoperable system. Heads rolled. It was an unplanned bonus. By this point Charlie was long gone, well on his way from the Gimbels parking lot and out of the Cross-County

Shopping Center complex. However, I could not think about Charlie. I had to act like I had been robbed.

Explaining with tears and terror in my voice, visibly shaken, repeating over and over, "I pressed the button, but nothing happened!" The barrage of questions from the guard stared. "What'd he look like? How tall was the guy? What kind of build's he have? You sure he had a gun? What'd the gun look like?"

I regurgitated the description of the convict on the Wanted Poster. Every detail committed to memory. Regarding the gun, I told them that the guy said he had one. Who was I to question him?

Another guard showed up, his breath, also reeked of alcohol. "Was he black, white? Can you tell us the color of the guy's hair? Any details?"

Shaking, I repeated, "It happened so fast! I was scared!"

The guards got on their radios and scrambled about. "Here sit down, are you ok? You want some water?"

According to the clock on the wall, it was then after closing.

Someone asked, "How do you usually get home? Does someone pick you up?"

"I walk. I don't live too far from here," was my reply and the truth.

"We'll call you a cab. Sometime tomorrow we'll need you to go downtown to the Police Station to give a statement."

I was escorted out the main door. There in the dark after closing was a waiting cab. Security paid the driver up front.

Once I finally got home, Joann was still awake. We sat down on my daybed, where I told her I had just been robbed at Gimbels. She knew that Charlie and I were capable of anything. Hell, all of us were. She was the sultan's favorite, after all. She smiled and said, "Wow that's too bad Mare." She did not say anything else. She did not express any suspicions she may have had. For Joann, the only reality was what I had told her.

It was the unsaid that we all agreed and were bound by tribal loyalty. I slept amazingly well that night.

Chapter 9
Big Coat

The following morning, Super Bowl Sunday morning, as expected., Gimbels' Security called. "We need you to give a statement at the Police Station, the one on Locust Avenue. Can you be there by eleven? Ask for Sargent DeRosa. They just need a statement to complete the report we filed last night. OK?"

I decided the best person to call for a ride was my Father. Later I felt badly about lying to him, but that morning I needed him to be an uninformed dad. It was good for the image, a middle-class kid from a good family, her dad at her side. "She's a good student," he would say. "She works hard. She's supposed to go on a class trip this week for college credit." Dad would be the ultimate character witness. We did not speak much on the way to the Police Station.

Dad had helped my brothers out of plenty of jams. Now, it was my turn. The difference though was my brothers had confessed straight up to him. With them, Dad knew what he was getting into. My eldest brother had come home once after banging up his car, really badly. My Father and he went out with the car later that night. They drove it to the Grand Concourse in the Bronx and parked it under the L. They left the doors unlocked, the keys in the ignition, and took the train home. The car was reported stolen to the insurance company the next day.

As far as my father knew, I was robbed at gunpoint while working. All he could say about what happened to me was, "What's the world coming to? Yonkers is going down the tubes."

"The guy said he had a gun." The guy was the guy in the black and white photo I had lifted from the P.O.'s "Wanted" files. "So, I gave him the money." The Police Sergeant said I did the right thing. My father agreed.

Another policeman yelled over from an adjoining room, "Hey, hurry up in there. The game's gonna start soon! We gotta check out the stats."

I could see a TV on through the window divider. There was a big spread of food on the table - chips, dip, soda. The smell of barbequ cooking was coming in from behind the building.

The Sergeant had me sit down at a large table. He dropped a huge dusty book of "Wanted" photos in front of me. He said I needed to look through the book to see if I recognized 'my guy.' I sat alone, turning the pages slowly, while my dad and the officer chatted in ear shot.

My Dad was telling the Sergeant what a good student I was. How hard I worked. How art school had always been my dream.

"Okay," I shouted. I had finished the book. My guy was not in it! Tears started running down my face.

The officer and my father came back to where I was sitting. In their eyes, I was a victim and a daughter, understandably disturbed by a startling crime. "Don't worry," the officer said. "He won't hurt you. You're finished now. Your Dad can take you home."

I was crying because of what I had overhead. I never imagined that my Dad knew or cared about my dreams, not until that moment. Now that I knew he clearly did care, I could not stop bawling. However, I could not go soft. It was of absolute importance that my Dad remain in the dark, clueless about the money I stole, money that would help pay for some of my dreams.

A perk of working at Gimbels was the twenty percent discount you received on purchases. Most kids working there spent a huge amount of their paycheck on clothes. They were the stylishly dressed kids. All you had to do was put some money down from each week's paycheck, set it on layaway and once paid off, the clothes would be yours. The fashion-conscious, trendy kids worked to give their pay right back to the store for the latest Calvin Klein jeans and being Gimbels, the brands were more upscale than the affordable small shops. These kids were spending their money on names like Halston, Yves Saint Laurent, real leather shoulder bags and high platform shoes.

Ordinarily I avoided buying anything at Gimbels. I had more important things to spend my money on than their up-market flared jeans. Once I did purchase paint from the Craft Department, on the lower level, next to Stamp Collecting. Even with the discount, the paint was expensive. I never would have bought it there, except I had run out of paint and needed some right away for a project due at RCC. I could not wait to go to the more affordable art supply store in Mount Vernon.

Only once did I make use of Gimbels' layaway. One day after I punched in, rushed up past perfume and shoes, around the corner, then up the escalator, I saw IT. IT was boldly displayed on a manne-quin, at the top of the escalator - a soft, buttery-to-touch suede coat.

It was the color of sepia, mid-calf, tailored with darts at the waist and flared at the bottom. The collar was faux fur of the same color, and when I tried it on, you could not tell where the collar started, and my hair ended. It was belted and lined with an equally smooth gold satin. IT I would buy. I finished paying off the coat just in time to wear it on my first trip to Europe, to London.

Two days after Super Bowl Sunday, three days after we took the Gimbels' money, I was on my way to the airport, to catch my flight to London. One of the guys from Charlie's band, Johnny, had offered to give me a ride to Kennedy Airport.

Wearing my new sepia suede coat, feeling triumphant, I walked through security, my passport in hand. I checked my suitcase in and lit up the cigar Johnny had given me. The guys from the band had all heard about what Charlie and I had 'possibly' done. Nobody asked, nobody spoke about it. That was the unwritten rule. Johnny had handed me the cigar as he lifted my luggage out of the car. "Enjoy your trip man," was all he said; then he kissed me on the cheek. Inside the airport, I met the other art students who were flying to London. They had traveled together to by bus from Rockland County to Kennedy Airport.

Chapter 10
Escape

Time in London flew by. I felt all the newness of the experience and was elated to be there. After arrival and after checking into our hotel, everyone slept to catch up on the time difference. But my brain was not going to shut off enough to allow for sleep.

That first night I wandered off by myself, finding my way through the streets of London, completely carefree. Nobody to answer to, no questions directed at me, no looking over my shoulder. London's streets were laid out so differently from the grid of New York City. It took some getting used to find my way around. The scale of the buildings, the lights, and, oh, the driving! My left and right street crossings became something I had to plan. London was the best escape in 1973, I loved being surrounded by people with British accents. I loved seeing all the street punks with their green Mohawks, safety pin piercings, chains, leather, and Doc Martins. Most of all I loved the small bookshops loaded with incredibly old books. They were the best escape. The London Underground - also known as the 'tubes' - was easy to navigate, much easier than New York City's subway. I loved being sucked deep into its maze.

I let myself escape from my native lifestyle into a culture I had previously only read of or heard about. Being in London allowed me to reinvent myself. Here I was free of all the entanglements I had just left, no looking over my shoulder, no worries of suspicion. Here I could immerse myself as an art student without a care. I was aware of only museums, collections, and artists. The entire experience changed me. My eyes began to examine paintings with new focus.

Back home in Yonkers, I would often find my way to New York City to the Museum of Modern Art or the Metropolitan Museum of Art. But in London, a new maturity set in. Maybe it was because my heart and mind were more capable of empathy or I had simply become more open to the artist's intent. No matter the reason, the effect would last a lifetime. Without he distraction of life in Yonkers, for the first time in my life I felt like my dream of becoming an artist was in reach. Being beyond the influences of Yonkers made me feel new, awakened, I saw paintings with fresh eyes and open heart. I could be an artist, there was nobody in England to say otherwise. None of the voices of my parents or friend who didn't understand saying, "You can't make a living as an artist, don't waste time and money on studying art." With this freedom of experiencing who I was, an awakening of wholeness about painting and art settled into my being. Art and its purpose engulfed me and with that enlightenment I became awed at a diversity that I had never understood before. This trip to England, visiting all these museums, seeing all that history, was the validation I had been seeking.

I drew the puzzle pieces of Greek figures that make up the Elgin Marbles at he Britsh Museum and recognized that if there ever was a way to time travel, artists had figured it out.

Rembrandt's "Self Portrait with Two Circles" circled my mind. He was sitting right there in the same room with me, his eyes fixed into my soul. DaVinci's "Madonna of the Rocks" stretches out her hands to touch me as I passed; she was serene and organic. The light from within it is Leonardo's hand, the painter reaching out to grab the viewer. Francis Bacon's triptych of an isolated figure struck me as fully modern symbolism; it had the presence of something in motion. At the Courtauld Institute of Art I saw Manet's "A Bar at Folies-Bergère". Here I met the barmaid who stands between two worlds. The girl is a reflection and yet not a reflection. I know this girl. I know her well. I stood in front of her mesmerized for the longest time.

After ten days of life-changing joy, I returned to my wretched life in Yonkers, which still included the job at Gimbels. I figured that for the time being, I had to continue working there to reinforce my innocence. It was no surprise that Gimbels reorganized their Refund Policy Procedures. We could no longer dole out cash in "Gift Wrapping." A couple of kids from other departments did make some snide remarks to me insinuating that I probably robbed myself, but nothing stuck. The ladies I worked with refrained from even mentioning the incident for fear of traumatizing me further.

I had also decided I would permanently be leaving Yonkers, sooner rather than later.

Chapter 11
Debt paid

Within two weeks of returning from London, Charlie dropped in at the apartment Joann and I shared. He came by late when he knew I would be home from work. He had a brown paper bag with him. I told him about London, and he spoke of how he had managed to keep himself isolated while I was away. He had gone on a heroin binge. He was basically stoned the entire time I was out of the country. He said he felt safe in the unworldliness of a heroin that while he was in that place, he would not reveal anything to anybody.

Inside the brown paper bag was the package I had last seen him holding, exactly as I had handed it to him. The wrapping paper and trinket on top tied into the bow were all still intact. As we unwrapped it, I asked him where he had stashed it. Charlie looked up in between licking papers and said, "In a hole in the tree in the front yard of my parent's house."

A hollow in a tree. I had an image of a modern-day Zarathustra *'When the morning dawned, however, Zarathustra found himself in a thick forest, and no path was any longer visible. He then put the dead man in a hollow tree at his head- for he wanted to protect him from the wolves- and laid down on the ground and moss. And immediately he fell asleep, tired in body, but with a tranquil soul.*" from Thus Spoke Zarathustra. So here was Charlie while I was gone stuffing a box instead of a body into the cavity of a hollow tree to protect it from wolves and then dozing off into a tranquil heroin sleep. We split the money equally. Charlie left that night and went off to bury himself in a recording studio on the Yonkers-Bronx border to mix and cut his very own CD of original songs.

Charlie came to see me again a few weeks later. He was excited about the recording. It was going well, and he seemed more alive than I could remember him being in a long time. He asked if he could borrow another five hundred dollars. He said he was short that amount to complete the studio sessions. "Sure, why not," I said. I had it to give. "Pay me back when you can."

In the fall, I registered for the semester at Rockland Community College. After filling out endless papers, schedules and standing in long lines, I handed the clerk at the Bursars' Office the cost of my tuition in small bills. She started counting, then looked up and said, "Honey you must have been saving up for a while."

With a big smile, I said, "Yep, every penny I could get my hands on!"

What made me assume I could get away with what I had done?

Every day that passed without incident, made me feel increasingly confident that I had indeed gotten away with larceny. However, I knew I could not rely on luck forever. What I had done necessitated a change. I decided I had to quit Gimbels. I would leave during spring break. Most of the college kids working at the store, went away during spring break to party in Florida; in most cases, after two weeks of sun, sea, sex and binge drinking they rarely returned to their jobs. I would also leave and not return. I would give notice that week. The managers would be scrambling to fill all the positions vacated by the college part-timers. I would go unnoticed as part of the youthful exodus.

That spring, after leaving Gimbels, I would also leave Yonkers. It was time to move out and move on. I had a nagging suspicion that if I stayed in Yonkers I would end up in jail or dead. I had too much to do with my life. Art and painting were calling me to be elsewhere.

I did not have much to pack, as I did not own much. Some clothes and art supplies, that was it. I had secured a place to live with a fellow art student at RCC who needed a roommate. That April, Charlie came to see me one last time before I relocated. He was working part time as a bike courier in New York City. How he got the job was beyond me, but that is how he was supporting himself. He said he couldn't pay me the five hundred dollars I had lent him to finish his recording, but he thought he had something I might accept in exchange.

"I guess it depends on what you've got."

I hoped it was not drugs. I was in the process of making a lot of changes. Included in the changes was eliminating drugs. He pulled out a shopping bag that contained six reels of what looked to be film footage. He said he found the reels in a dumpster in the city one day, during his courier travels.

"You'd be surprised at the stuff people throw out." Charlie knew how much I admired John Lennon. The reels of film footage were of John Lennon. Charlie said they might be worth something.

I did admire John Lennon. Hell, I adored the man, his music, his wit, his stand on war, his creative mind. I had gone to his concert at Madison Square Garden, the peace rallies with Yoko and David Peel. I could even recite his poems. "I sat belonely down a tree, humble, fat and small."

I told Charlie, "Sure, why not, consider the debt paid," with that he handed me the reels. From what I could tell they were all sixteen-millimeter footage of John Lennon, one large reel and several smaller ones.

Charlie said he was headed to Arizona. His band Saphire had secured a number of gigs out west through their drummer, a kid named Tom but we always addressed him as Oh Tom, who had once lived in Phoenix. He would be leaving in a couple of weeks. Charlie said, "Mare why don't you come out there with me? We could get married."

His words were totally unexpected. I held my breath, wondering how I should respond. I certainly trusted Charlie, but did I love him? I felt he knew my soul and that seemed good enough. His proposal was only slightly tempting. "I can't leave," I said, "not yet. I have to finish school." I had made a promise to myself that above all I would finish school.

He understood. "OK, well why don't we get married when I get back then?"

"Yea, that sounds like a plan."

We promised to write each other while he was away, and come fall, we would be reunited. We did write, every week, and every week I told myself I was not alone. I would write to Charlie about life in Rockland County, the hiking and swimming in the lakes. I wrote him letters about designs and paintings. I wrote and told him I was planning to transfer to Pratt in Brooklyn to study film.

I read his letters about the desert, the big sky, and how their drummer, Oh Tom, had missed a gig because he had taken off with a Mexican girl. Charlie wrote that they replaced him with a guy pulled from the audience at one of their shows. Charlie would periodically remind me of our plans to marry once he got back east. His letters filled an emotional void. They represented hope and something to which I could look forward.

In early fall, Charlie's letters became less frequent. He was supposed to return in late fall. He wrote to say he would not be back until late November, hopefully, before Thanksgiving. In November, the letters stopped all together. Frantic for any information about him, I called Skip. Skip was clueless. He was upstate in Oneonta, out of touch with goings on in Arizona. I heard no further word from anyone. Nothing. Then, in the dismal grayness of January, while home on break, Skip called. "Hey babe, I scored you a ticket for the Who concert at Madison Square Garden. Meet me at the diner on McLean Avenue. You can ride with us."

"I'm in! What time?"

"We'll pick you up there at six." Then Skip dropped a bomb on me. "Oh, and get this, Charlie, the funk master, will be back two days before the concert. Man, he got himself hitched! Can you believe it? What the fuck! I told him I only had a ticket for him, not tickets for him and his bitch."

"What are you talking about?" I tried to hide my shock.

Charlie and I had not told anyone about our plan to marry when he returned from the west. It was our plan, just between us. Like so many other things, we kept it secret. Skip did not know our plan, but he did know that Charlie would be back and that he was married. I felt kicked in the gut. Charlie had married someone else.

Charlie and I had done a lot of walking in Yonkers. It is a walkable city, easy to get around without a car, and walking meant one less expense. I grew up on a dead-end street and learned street smarts from being in a dead-end culture with dead end jobs in dead end Yonkers.

learned that when you come to a dead end, there is nothing left to do but turn around and take another road.

Surrealist portrait of Charlie 1974

Part 2

In the end life catches up and time steals us away.
We become a footnote in the passing.
The stars look down on us and laugh at our temporary status.
They have stolen our light and know more than we do.

Chapter 12
Twenty-five Years

Charlie was wrong. We did not have to grow up and become our parents. Since we knew better, we could do better. When we were young, hanging around in Yonkers, Charlie and I often talked about how horrible our parents were - how they didn't understand us, how they wanted us to be something other than what we wanted to be, how we couldn't talk to them. Mostly, we talked about how angry they would get.

Charlie would say, "You'll see, someday our kids will hate us as much as we hate our folks. It's just the way it is. Every generation resents the previous one."

But he was wrong.

I did not allow my family history to play out like a broken record.

Instead, I smashed that record. I raised my daughter by my instincts, by what I knew to be right. I raised her with lots of love, attention, and laughter.

Circumstances, life, and love led me to being a single mom.

My life after Yonkers orbited around Rockland Community College's Art Department. I did some work while there tutoring students on woodcut printing after studying for a year at Pratt Institute's Film School in Brooklyn, New York. Getting accepted into Pratt was the easy part, I sat on a park bench in New York's Central Park thinking where the hell am I going to live? As fate would have it I pulled out a matchbook with the name and address on it. A kid I knew from RCC, also an art student, had given it to me after the last semester at RCC. He said, "If you're ever in New York, look me up," and Jimmy wrote down where he'd be. I took the chance and walked down to 92nd St between 1st and 2nd, found his building and within no time was moving in, sharing space in his railroad apartment. Jimmy carved out a room for me between the kitchen and his bedroom and along with another kid, Jack, who got the couch in the living room, the three of us shared the rent. The commute to Brooklyn from Manhattan was a simple train ride. I had decided to major in filmmaking. Film represented a powerful medium to me, especially since my experience with the events that happened to me directly after watching *A Clockwork Orange*.

I was immersed in everything film, from history to editing, writing and shooting. Film history was an evening class, we watched classics like "Grand Illusion" and modern minimalists where the camera simply panned in on a photograph on a wall for thirty minuets. Most of us in that class caught on quickly and brought pop-corn, snacks and joints to smoke to class.

I spent two months in the editing room slicing footage I had shot for my final project. I recruited a friend from Yonkers, Dean, an aspiring actor, to star in my film project. He worked full time in his family tradition as a firer fighter, but his passion was acting. Dean was delighted to be my star performer. We shot some footage of him in his Greenwich Village apartment, scene one, Dean sitting at his kitchen table drinking coffee in front of the window that looked out to the roof, scene two, Dean on the roof prancing around deliberately stepping over and into a wooden frame. I decided to splice the two different scenes together based on the mathematical formula known as the Golden Section. This meant the ratio and proportion of each scene was calculated out, cut accordingly and sliced back together until they merged in the middle of the film. Esoteric and tedious and before the age of computers, I spent hours upon hours manually editing a five minute film. The most frustrating part was that, unlike the wealthy kids from Long Island, I did not have money to buy the necessary cocaine needed to bribe the technicians who were there to assist us. I completed my piece alone and received accolades from the faculty but I knew the film industry was too expensive for me, I'd go back to painting after this semester and finalized my education with a degree in Art History.

Bribing at Pratt reached it's pinnacle a few years later when in '78 a film crew bribed a janitor to allow them to use the library and gym locker rooms for production. The result, which I'm sure the janitor never expected, was a widely successful, for it's time, pornographic film we know as *Debbie Does Dallas*. Needless to say the janitor lost his job.

However, the real-life changer for me was marrying one of my former RCC art professors. He was twenty years my senior. Marrying an older man was characteristic of my rebellious tendencies. We were a bohemian couple. Artists, intellectuals, educators, and historians of all disciplines surrounded us.

We settled into a two story Garden apartment in Spring Valley not far from the college. Our living room space was used as a studio, packed with paintings, art supplies, easels, plants and cheap oriental rugs covering the floors. We entertained faculty with rowdy evenings drinking, singing and limerick challenges that were bawdy and drunken. The walls were paper thin and the sounds of grunting and thumping drifted through from the apartment next to ours belonging to a gay couple there. We entertained ourselves by speculating on what went beyond those walls next door. Eventually there was a demonstrative lovers quarrel, first one moved out slamming the door and then days later the other fellow parted. The apartment maintaince came around to clean the place out after no one returned calls to claim their stuff. I ran into the super cleaning up in the hallway, he said, "Wow, you should see the stuff they left behind." My curiosity was already lit so I went in, pocked my head into the room where I was expecting to see what bizarre sexually apparatus they had, instead I discovered that they used the space as a workout room with all kinds of weights, and equipment, so much for all that thumping and grunting.

As our marriage grew so did our needs and we brought a small old farmhouse in Orange County with a half hour commute to the college. This bucolic setting came established with barns and outbuildings that served as studio, plenty of room for storage and a great place to raise a child. This is where I still live today.

Meanwhile, always in the back of my mind, stashed away, hidden in a closet in my bedroom was the handful of 16mm reels of film footage from one of the most prolific musicians of my generation. John Lennon had redefined music as we knew it, throughout his career, both during and after the Beatles.

"Wait twenty-five years." Brown Adams, the historian, told me. He said, "I suggest you put this film footage of John Lennon away and forget about it. The statute of limitations for film, for outright ownership, is twenty-five years. After that, you'll be able to sell the reels, free and clear."

Twenty-five years is a long time, especially when you are only twenty-five-years-old yourself.

Brown was the definitive voice of silent films. Brown was a retired film historian who now gave talks and lectures on film as part of the extensive cultural arts program sponsored by the college. It was a non-credit program opened to the general public, with free admission usually scheduled on Friday evenings and held at an off campus site in Nyack, close to where Brown lived. He had the largest private collection of authentic reels of silent film in the New York metropolitan area. He was a walking encyclopedia of knowledge on all things cinematic. My husband and I regularly attended his Friday evening film series at the college and became familiar with classics such as Birth of a Nation and early Surrealists works.

I must admit, it was a relief to hear from Brown Adams that I should store the footage. In my heart, I did not want to be another person capitalizing on a death. I was angry and shocked when I heard the news. We did not have a TV at our apartment, so when we walked to work on the morning following his death, I was not sure at first why students and staff were crying.

"Did you hear, how awful?"

"When is this kind of thing going to stop? Why kill John Lennon?"

Why? Is there something hot wired into our DNA that makes us so aggressive and destructive? Will we eventually annihilate ourselves completely? I do not know, but on December 8, 1980 John Lennon was gunned down outside his apartment at the Dakota in New York

City, the city he loved.

It is now 1997 and I am looking for the film footage of John Lennon that I had stored away over twenty- five years ago. I have spent the entire day emptying the contents of my closets. It is time for my daughter to apply to colleges. I was able to eke out a decent living wage since divorcing my husband, securing independence for myself and my daughter. We did not have a lot, but we had enough. I swore that I would make sure she would be able to go to college without the grief getting a college education had incurred on me at her age. I believed my film footage of John Lennon would make my dream for my daughter possible.

Your past rolls past you, your present captures a today, and then catapults you into your future. It all happens so fast, yet it can feel like you are just crawling along slowly.

Chapter 13
Last Call

Art is art. Painting was my world and my life, but as my eleven-year marriage began to teeter, I realized I had a child to support and a household to manage. Things would have to change. I was living with an alcoholic. Unfortunately, three years of combined marriage counseling, rehab and individual therapy did not overcome my soon-to-be ex-husband's destructive behavior and its aftershocks. I was exhausted from trying to make the marriage work. In my heart I knew it was over, and having left drugs and Yonkers behind me years ago, there was no way I could continue with a miserable marriage. I was not raising my daughter Gabriella in an environment where we had to tiptoe around a dominating and destructive drinker. We deserved better, and as difficult as it might be, my daughter and I would be better off on our own. The decision was made.

My husband's alcoholism permeated our household. It increased gradually from not so noticeable social drinking to flat out opening a bottle of cheap Philly Scotch Whiskey at 11am on Saturday mornings, passing out by three in the afternoon, waking up and starting all over again at dinner time. That was excessive. Like any good alcoholic, my "professor" husband functioned well at work. Nobody at the workplace could imagine how privately dysfunctional he was domestically. Maybe they suspected, but since they all worked for him, nobody spoke a word of it.

Over the years I had watched how drinking was his means of dealing with stress and coping with the crap life throws at you. Under the circumstances, I found myself becoming protective of my own thoughts and emotions. I began to close my heart to him and isolate myself from his behavior. At the same time, I was also guarding our daughter from his volatile actions and words.

I had never known someone who abused alcohol. Drug addicts I could deal with. I had certainly know enough of them, enough to know not to marry one. Sadly, it seemed the alcoholism slowly crept up with my husband. At first, I overlooked the obvious. In my mind I excused his behavior, expecting things to improve. Soon I was mindful of every move I made around him.

Unfortunately, the downward spiral just continued until I reached my breaking point. It took all my courage and resolve to confront my husband, the man who had been my mentor, and who I thought was wiser than me, since he was older and more experienced.

Once the words came out - "I think you need help with your drinking. You're an alcoholic" - the avalanche of events could not be halted. We tumbled through three years of bickering, therapy, and counseling until, ultimately, he agreed to rehab.

We mutually decided he would go during the summer months. He wanted anonymity, to maintain his privacy at the college. I could understand that. The summer he was away were the most peaceful six weeks I had experienced in years. My daughter and I managed the household. I picked up some freelance graphic work, and we enjoyed our freedom. We did not have to walk-on-eggshells. That alone relieved a tremendous amount of stress. During my husband's stay in rehab, I realized how much I missed the intelligent man I had married, not the alcoholic he had become. I had no idea what to expect when he returned.

We occasionally spoke on the phone during his absence. Once, in his desperation to do the right thing, he said, "I promise you anything, anything you want to make it up to you."

"A honeymoon," was my response. We had never gone on a honeymoon, having been married on a whim by a local justice of the peace. I wanted us to go on a honeymoon. This could be the fresh start we needed.

When he was finished with rehab, his larger than life personality, tenacity and dramatics came home, and once again he dominated the household. Now, we were tiptoeing around his recovery needs. He was sober but he was also incredibly angry. Angry at me, his young wife, for telling him he was an alcoholic.

The honeymoon never happened, in fact, he never brought it up again. Seven months later, when my birthday rolled around, I said, "Maybe we can plan our honeymoon." He glared at me. I immediately felt his dark black eyes burning through me. He said nothing, reached into his pocket, and pulled out a small box wrapped in neat silver paper. He threw the tiny prize at me with all the intensity of the piercing anger in his eyes. It landed under the table. In an instant, I recalled the story he used to tell of how he had once thrown a waitress her tip to make her crawl for it. He thought she had been provoking him; he was probably drunk at the time. Now he was throwing my birthday present at me, expecting me to crawl for it. I did. I crawled under the table, picked up the box, and carefully unwrapped it. Inside was a gold ring with five small diamonds, set in a heart shape. I placed it on my finger, and with my eyes focused on his still stabbing gaze locked on me , I said, "I want a divorce."

Then and there, after three years of working to keep the marriage going, I realized I had had enough. I was ready to move on. I had strengthened myself while he was away and knew I could provide a better environment for myself and my daughter. It might be difficult, but I was not afraid of the challenge. I would figure it out somehow. I would wear his ring and refer to it as my divorce ring.

My annual income in 1989 went from $87,000, as a married woman whose salary was jointly combined with her husband's, to $17,000 as a single mom. My now ex-husband was well versed in matters concerning divorce. I was his third wife, and as far as any support went, he begrudgingly granted me the minimum in child support. I told myself, "It's ok. we'll manage." And we did. Gabriella and I did not have a lot, but we were creative and had laughter and friends; our endurance became our bond.

To move forward I needed to find steady work, full-time employment. Freelance design work would not cut it. There were too many monthly bills to pay, health insurance, and now someone else's future to consider. Sustaining my daughter and I on the sale of my paintings would not be enough. I needed financial stability

What better job for a single mom but working the nightshift. After securing the position, I placed an ad in the Help Wanted for a babysitter indicating the evening hour needed. Carol was the first person I interviewed, she live in the next town over, also a single mom in her fifties, her own daughter being in her mid-twenties. Carol was a down-to-earth tough cookie with a great laugh. She worked a full-time job from 2am to 9am, she was looking for extra work and said our hours would fill her schedule well. The arrangement worked

ell, Carol would get to our house fifteen minuets before I left at
:15 after Gabriella and I had our dinner. Gabriella and we both felt
omfortable with her as part of our family. We set up a bed for Carol
ı our extra room so she could sleep. Carol would set her alarm for
45 and in the silent hours of the morning as I was coming in, Carol
ould then leave for her other job. Along with Carol's experience and
eneral jovial nature this arrangement lasted for a good six years and
hen Carol could no longer for for us, her daughter took over. Need-
ss to say, we became mutual support for each other, celebrating
irthdays and holidays and our struggle as single mom families.

The local newspaper's night shift production team was Prepress
raphics. The job fit my needs with a steady income, benefits and,
ost importantly, time to be home with my daughter during the day.
he staff was predominantly female, and all but one was a single
om. There were also elderly matrons who could type with amazing
eed. It was all incredibly old school. Inputting the copy required for
e four nightly deadline editions created the circus that was the night
ift.

In the 1990's, newspaper production pre-press was a manual skill
f tedious cutting and pasting, with editors hanging over your shoul-
er. Cuts and additions were made on the fly to update stories before
ansmitting them to film and plate. The result was the morning
ewspaper, which landed on subscribers' doorsteps.

Production women were cut from independent cloth. They juggled
ds, households, jobs, and bills, to make ends meet. The night shift
litorial staff was markedly different. The staff were either ancient
coholics or young transient go-getters, do-gooders who still be-
ved in a journalistic mission to uncover the truth. The ones set on
career in journalism were fresh out of college with no life experi-
ce. After a year, they would move on to bigger metro papers with

higher paying salaries. Those who remained working the night shift shared a common bond - we were all misfits existing on the flip side of life.

Tabloid newspaper people were not like the academics I had come to know at RCC. The crew was brassy and practical. It performed with information streaming in and deadlines barking every hour. Everyone had to be decisive. The night crew drank beer at last call and played pool. There were no glasses of Chardonnay, no dinner parties no deans, or professors among the gang at Prepress Graphics. Headline writers, worked alongside a team of women who ran around wit sharp knives able to cut up stories, slap them down and move them out to press, in time for the paper's early morning edition.

It was only after I divorced my husband, that I recognized how insulated our academic world had been. Indeed, my experience at the newspaper differed from any work I had previously known. It was different. However, it was never dull. The work could be tedious at times, and, typical of tabloid presses, it could be tragic and ridiculous I entered the newspaper industry when it was still experiencing huge profit margins. In 1989, newspapers still led the way as the source of reliable information for the public. Regardless of the position you were hired for, folks on the night shift freely debated and gave their opinions about that evening's headlines. There were no filters on our personal comments. If we collectively met the deadline for going to press in the morning, the daytime management left us to our own devices. The nightshift newspaper staff was an example of controlle chaos. If everything went smoothly, we usually met one last deadlin That was at the last call at the local bar.

working nightshift as paste-up 1990

Chapter 14
A Scrap of Paper

Working nights in production, we had access to information from all over the world. Nightshift workers generally gravitated to macabre and weird storylines.

I figured it came with the label "graveyard shift."

A particular headline, under most people's radar, grabbed my eye. It had come in from the Detroit News, Thursday, January 23, 1997:

NEWSMAKERS: BEATLES AUCTION GOES WORLDWIDE.

Paul McCartney probably will not like what is going to happen March 22 in Tokyo.

That is when an auction house is going to put on what is being billed as the first international auction devoted entirely to Beatles' memorabilia. More than $1.6 million is expected to be bid for items ranging from a bass once owned by McCartney to the Liverpool house where Ringo Starr was born.

Bonhams Auction House says the sale will be beamed to an expected 25 million households across Europe by the new British-based cable Auction Channel. Viewers will be able to bid by telephone, fax, or internet. McCartney, who thinks the whole Beatle memorabilia business is out of hand, recently got an injunction to stop the private sale of a scrap of paper with the lyrics to "With A Little Help from My Friends".

I had more than a scrap of paper to sell.

Earlier in the day I was sitting on my porch drinking coffee in the radiant light of morning, the air fresh, the wind blowing through treetops, and everywhere birds were calling. The mockingbird was, and still is, my favorite.

I hate cleaning out a closet, but that day, that was exactly what I would be doing. There was stuff in the closet that I did not want to throw away because I was certain I would use it or wear it again. My Lennon films were there, tucked away somewhere in the back of the closet. I dug through layers of sweaters, fabrics, t-shirts, shoes, boots, sleeping bags, boxes of costume jewelry, mostly earrings, and at the bottom of the closet, in an old artist's portfolio, I found the reels of film.

You know what they say, strike when the iron is hot. Beatles' memorabilia was more than hot, it was on fire. The time had come to sell the films.

Thursday, January 23, 1997   **The Detroit News**

National news   ◄ **INDEX** ►

Newsmakers: Beatles auction goes worldwide

Paul McCartney probably won't like what's going to happen March 22 in Tokyo. That's when an auction house is going to put on what is being billed as the first international auction devoted entirely to Beatles memorabilia. More than $1.6 million is expected to be bid for items ranging from a bass once owned by McCartney to the Liverpool house where Ringo Starr was born. The Bonhams auction house said the sale would be beamed to an expected 25 million households across

---

Chapter 15
Copyrights

One thing I learned from my divorce was the importance of a good lawyer. So even before approaching anyone about selling my film footage, I searched for a lawyer. I found one in West Nyack - Mr.Furglough, an intellectual property rights lawyer. Sounded right. After a few calls, I booked an appointment and found myself, on a warm summer day, stepping into a sleek modern air-conditioned office building. I described the film I owned. I did not spell out the exact "How's" of my attaining it, just enough information to satisfy the lawyer's questions.

I told him, "It was a payback for money I had lent a friend who later found these outtakes in a dumpster in New York City." I felt comfortable asking questions myself and took notes. I found out where I stood as the owner of the footage, what was possible and why.

My film reels fell under the time-honored tradition of 'owner's keepers'. But what exactly did that mean? Mr. Furglough had explained that if the film was in my possession, I owned it. In other

ords, if I let the film out of my hands, it would belong to the
erson to whom I had given it. What I did not own was the image
f John Lennon. What this boiled down to was that I could sell the
lm footage outright, but I could not take any of the images of John
ennon and sell them on T-shirts, for example, or blow them up as
osters. Yoko Ono, or what is known as the Lennon estate, owned
hn's image. There was one other important point. I was clear to
ll the films "as is" because the film was made prior to the copyright
ws of 1977.

Mr. Furglough went on to explain about litigation that had oc-
urred in California in 1977. The visual artist Robert Rauschenberg
ot pissed at his gallery and punched a collector, in 1972. After the
cident, the collector made a huge profit on the reselling of one of
e artist's paintings. What made Rauschenberg angry was that he
d not get a penny of the profit on the resale. Rauschenberg filed a
wsuit and won 5% of the resale price of his own work. Rauschen-
erg's victory changed a lot of things for artists in all mediums, but it
nly applied to works sold after the successful lawsuit. The royalties
r copyright infringement and its effectiveness were disputed and
ounced around in the courts in several cases, including one against
auschenberg himself. Prior to 1972, artists' compensation did not
ist. According to Mr. Furglough, I could play it safe by selling
e film as is, or I could totally reconstruct the reels as another "art
rm" and risk a battle with the Lennon estate.

Possession is nine-tenths of the law. This information would prove
riceless in negotiation, and it was worth every penny I spent on my
nsultation with Mr. Furglough.

Chapter 16
Proceed with Caution

Initially, working nights felt like an escape from the daily routine of life. I did my food shopping after my shift at 2:00 a.m. at a twenty-four-hour supermarket. There were no crowds to deal with, just stock boys in the aisles. During the afternoons, there was always time for a doctor or dentist appointment. And I was available to be a chaperone for school trips, although, in my role as chaperone, I slept on the bus most of the time. There was also much needed time to spend in my studio. I hoped that if my paintings could talk, they'd say, "I like being alive, breathing in, smelling the grass, and feeling the sun kissing my eyelids. Did you see the blue sky today?" I did.

Free afternoons afforded me plenty of time to hang out at the coffee shop in my village. Most folks I met there worked freelance, in one capacity or another. They were designers, craftspeople, self-employed types. Our non-conformist revenue streams bonded us. Marie and her husband owned the coffee shop. Marie ran the shop, and her husband crafted wooden furniture in a studio in the rear. I enjoyed sitting in the shop, catching up with the regulars. There was Kevin and Morris who had their own freelance design business; Rachael who made jewelry and sold it at festivals; and Maggie, sweet Maggie, who ran a vintage antique shop and was a devoted Grateful Dead fan. She followed the band from concert to concert each summer, all over the northeast. Our group constituted the local creative/hippie element.

It was during a conversation one afternoon that I mentioned the article I'd seen about the Rock 'n Roll sale and how I might try to sell an item I owned.

"Has anyone ever heard of Bonhams Auction House? Anyone ever have experience selling items of memorabilia?"

Kevin jumped right in. He had come into possession of a deceased South American artist's work. Based on my own dealings with Kevin, I could only imagine how he had gotten his hands on the paintings. I did not even ask. I did not want to know. I described the films that I had in my possession. Kevin explained how he was selling images from the paintings on t-shirts and computer-generated prints pulled from the dead artist's work. Trouble was Kevin could not manage to sell the paintings outright. No gallery would touch them because Kevin could not prove possession with clear provenance.

He said, "Hey you could make some serious money selling t-shirts with images from the film. We could go in on it together. I'm all set up for that kind of work. I have connections with a head shop in Woodstock."

"No. no. no, I'm not going to sell any t-shirts with John Lennon's image on them." I made that clear to Kevin.

"Suit yourself," he snapped back.

I explained to him that t-shirts were not an option for me. "I'd get my ass sued by the Lennon estate if I were ever caught selling images of John Lennon."

Kevin gave me a look that asked, 'Are you too scarred, too dumb, or just a woman?'

"Come on Mare, how would Yoko know?"

I did not want to find out.

"Look, you talkin' Yoko? I got a book for you to read," he said, in a more serious and cautious tone, almost a whisper.

The only things I knew about Kevin were from the coffee shop. I knew he had a freelance graphics business with his partner Morris, who was at least a decade older than him. I knew he had a gallery in town selling t-shirts with Grateful Dead images, Indian mandalas, and goddesses; and I knew he lived upstairs from his shop in a loft. His girlfriend was a young girl from the local Ashram. He was quick to wheel and deal with anyone if he thought he could make a buck.

The next time I came into the shop, he pulled a book out of his knap-sack. "Read this. Check out the enemy." He passed the book to me as if it were a secret document. It was called *Last Days of John Lennon* by Fred Seaman. According to Kevin, there was "a lot of shit going down."

I could not stop reading. Fred Seaman was an ex-aid of John Lennon. After Lennon's shocking murder, Seaman wrote a not-so-pretty account of dealings with Yoko before and after John. Seaman made it his mission to discredit Yoko by portraying her as a questionable character.

I had always admired the woman, especially her early happenings, what is now referred to as "performance artist." She was a pioneering member of the Fluxus group, known for pieces that encouraged the audience to interact with her. In one well-known piece, she sat on a stage in a gown with a pair of scissors at her side, welcoming people to come up and cut off pieces of the gown. Her performance was considered a success, once the gown had been completely cut away, leaving a naked Yoko on the stage.

I was not sure how much of Seaman's book was true, but, after reading it, I decided I should proceed with caution.

Chapter 17
On Screen

In all the years of possessing the reels of Lennon film, I had viewed them only once. When Charlie first gave them to me, we rustled up a projector and watched them. A lot of time had passed since then, and I did not exactly remember what the films were about.

It was then 1998, and I wondered who would have a projector for 16mm film. I thought about it and went back to a reliable source, Rockland Community College. I thought of my old mentor, Brown Adams, showing films at RCC. If the college still had a film library, they would be sure to have a projector. I made calls to some old connections, and was put in touch with Roger. I remembered him from my early days at the college. He had been an intern in the film library, assisting Brown.

"Do you remember me?"

"Yes."

In an abridged version of my story, I explained how I had footage of John Lennon and wanted to sell it, but first I needed to view it and et a copy made.

Roger said, "Sure, sounds great, bring it down. You know we're all et up here and I can do one better. We can make a video copy for ou while you're here."

A few weeks later I found Roger's office at the college. It was here I had last seen him. He was in the basement of the library, ith not much in the way of windows, and shelves full of film, vid-os, and books.

Roger had thick glasses, a bearded long face, and moved with recise and deliberate gestures. I was not sure if years of handling elicate film had generated the way he moved, or if he was just that ay. He loaded the first reel, dimmed the lights, and John Lennon ap-eared, live on screen. We watched the spirit of John as he came to fe in front of us. Neither of us said a word. After the initial awe-ruck moments passed, Roger and I got down to business. I watched d took notes on the scenes and locations as Roger had suggested. oger kept count of the screen time on each reel. The film contents f John in New York City showed the legend:

- Dancing in Central Park at the bandstand
- Getting Italian ice from a street vendor
- Playing three card Monty in front of Tiffany's
- Smiling in a horse drawn carriage
- Strutting with his big, rimmed feather hat
- In his office twisting the shit out of a paper clip while having a onversation on the phone

These were outtakes. Roger then told me that D.A. Pennebaker, e folks who shot the footage of the Monterey Pop Festival, once ld him that they made more money on their outtakes of the docu-entary than the final theatre version. I was encouraged by that

81

tidbit of information. I left with my film and three videos copies. Thank you, Roger. He refused to take anything for his work. He said it was a pleasure to see unreleased images of John Lennon in private moments.

My next move was clear.

Chapter 18
Bonhams

July 20, 1997
Mr. Ted Owen
Bonhams
65 Lots Rd.
London, SW10,
England

Dear Mr. Owen,
As a follow up to our phone conversation, you will find the enclosed videotape which is a transfer of a cross section of the original 16mm film shot of John Lennon.

The small number of people who have seen this footage have responded with enthusiasm. The film itself consists of various 16mm, color clips, purchased in 1974. The footage had been shot in 1973 of and around John Lennon, set in different locations throughout New York City. The film sequences are outtakes and cutting room floor material. Similar shots where edited into promotional video *releases of the "Mind Games" and "Whatever Gets You through the Night" singles. Some of the scenes, particularly the close-ups of John on the phone, have not been seen even by the most ardent "Lennon aficionados."*

The film's total time is 45 minutes in length, originally consisting of hundreds of individual pieces. It has been rough edited into the below categories. There is also a four-five-minute section of raw NYC street scenes, acquired at the same time, with John likely on the other side of the camera.

CATEGORIES
- in Central Park
- at the bandstand
- with Yo-Yo man on the street
- at Sergeant Pepper's Way street
- at the Beacon theatre
- playing organ
- horse and carriage
- at the zoo
- signing autographs
- miscellaneous
Please contact me when you receive this package.
Yours truly,
Mary Altobelli

Things moved quickly. After the initial exchange of letters, I was soon on a phone call with Bonhams' London branch working out several details, dates, and confirmations. We were a go. Now it was necessary to make plans for delivery of the film to London. What better way to do so than in person?

I was thrilled to be telling my daughter that she and I would be taking a trip to London. This would be her first trip outside the U.S. I could not imagine a more appropriate reason for bringing her to my favorite city, a place that represented so much to me when I was her age. "We are going to deliver the reels of film personally." Bonhams was anxious to include them in their upcoming Beatles' memorabilia auction that Spring. My daughter and I were excited. We eagerly started planning our trip.

The auction was set for February 18, 1998. Bonhams required that the film be in-house a month prior to that date. They needed it in time to include the film in their promotional materials, auction brochure and general advertising for the auction. Winter break at school in January seemed the perfect time for us to travel. Airline tickets were reasonably priced, as winter was not exactly tourist season. We spread out maps of London and its underground across our living room floor, along with a London travel guidebook. Gabriella made a chart of the London sites we were interested in visiting, the streets they were on, the underground tube from our hotel to the sites, and the hours they were open. Together we plotted a great itinerary.

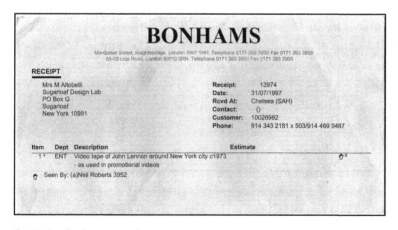

Receipt from Bonhams auction house

Chapter 19
Magic

We had scheduled four nights and five days, flying from Kennedy Airport in New York to Heathrow. We set out with bus tickets to Grand Central then onward to Kennedy Airport. The only thing enjoyable about waiting in an airport is people-watching. We focused on a group of men dressed in tunics who surprised us by rolling out little rugs and bending down in what we presumed was prayer. There was a beautiful little girl outfitted in traditional African prints, she was a princess doll. Once boarded on our international flight, there was a multitude of accents to overhear. We were flying Virgin Atlantic Airways to Heathrow, my second trip and Gabriella's first. I had suggested that we carry the film on our flight, in its original artist portfolio. Gabriella thought this was a good idea since this way we would not let it out of our sight. She offered to paint a peace sign on the outside and said we would take it on the flight as if it were a briefcase that James Bond needed to transport to high-level agents. To bring good fortune, she wore a special bracelet, which she had

ade. The future of her college education was in her carry-on. We
ere on a mission to deliver it to Ted Owen at Bonhams.

Upon arrival, we hopped on the underground and took it directly to
ur Russell Square hotel.

First and foremost, I notified Bonhams. We planned to be at their
Chelsea location soon after we arrived. We would take care of busi-
ess first then have the freedom to goof off, relax and enjoy the rest
f our time, taking in all the places we were so looking forward to
isiting.

The Chelsea District, where Bonhams is located, was new to me.
: was a vast collage of shops with antiques from around the world.
he auction house itself seemed to be a museum with the variety and
ge of the items it housed.

I asked the women behind the front desk for Ted Owens. Maybe it
as the jet lag, but I was jabbering away about our journey and how
iteresting this section of London was; when I stopped to catch my
reath, she said, "You must be Miss Altobelli from New York." For
he first time in my life I heard myself sounding like a "New Yorker."
laughed. I sounded like a foreigner even to myself. I could tell by
er look that I spoke way too fast and seemed comical. I realized
ow stereotypical my New York mannerisms must have seemed to
er.

A middle-aged man with gentle grey hair poked out of the office
ehind her and introduced himself. "Mary we are so glad to see you."
veryone was polite and Ted gave us a tour. He spent most of the
iorning with us, and I realized, unlike New Yorkers, Londoners were
ot in a hurry. He thanked us for trusting them with the sale of our
lm and told us it was the second highest priced piece in this year's
iction. One of John Lennon's pianos was the first item listed. He

gave me the price list, which included a listing for the film. He would also email me the information so that I could follow the auction live online from home.

After delivering our prized possession to its destination, we spent our first evening in London strolling through Piccadilly Circus and Tower Records. The itinerary we created was tight, we wanted to be as efficient as possible. To do so, we had marked desired sites in proximity to each other.

I had booked us a room at a hotel on Russell Square, near The British Museum. Like New York's Metropolitan Museum, The British Museum has an enormous collection, and it is impossible to absorb it all in one day. My thinking was to start each day by passing through a different section, on our way to that day's destinations. The museum did not disappoint. It is magic to be able to breathe in history though art. I could not have imagined the overwhelming sense of purpose that I experienced when I entered the Elgin Marbles with my daughter. Her immediate response was to take out her sketchbook and draw the sculptures. My eyes welled-up, as she did so. For a split second, I saw myself standing there next to Edgar as a young student. I had had the exact same response some thirty years earlier. Now, as I watched my daughter, I realized the torch had been passed.

One early morning we ventured to the Tower of London. The sun was blasting its ancient walls, as we mounted the stairs. Big black crows stood guard, while we spied diamonds to knock your eyes out. Outside at the tube station there was a life-sized sundial and more stairs. We hit Shakespeare's Globe Theatre and took the official tour and learned that the newly reconstructed theatre was opened in 1997. The replica a beautiful and precise structure located close to the original site with details that included enormous wooden beams and crushed hazelnut shells coating the earth ground where specta-tors stood for performances. Walking through the guided tour gave us a true sense of the excitement and entertainment experienced as Shakespeare would have provided his audiences.

The efficiency of our itinerary allowed us to maximize sites vis-ited in such a compact time frame. We had lunch on the Thames in the Greenwich Park area. We avoided the tourist type places and often walked down side streets where smaller local eateries were to be found. The pub we stumbled into was dark with low ceilings, a wooden structure and an older clientele all with pints in hand. Lunch included lentils, beef broth, and a sandwich; it was nothing like we would get back in the states. Later we checked out the Cutty Sark Maritime Museum then headed over to the Royal Observatory in Greenwich, standing at 00 or what is known as prime meridian, Greenwich Mean Time. My daughter shared not only my artistic endeavors but also a fascination with history and stargazing. The Observatory was the first institution that set the standard of naviga-tion in the sixteen hundreds. As museums go, it was fascinating, the early time devises for measurements, astronomical instruments, gears, wheels and telescopes all designed for making star positions to travel by.

We climbed more stairs than I knew possible. 540 spiraling up to the top of the dome at St Paul's Cathedral alone! Designed by Sir Christopher Wren, the stairs were well worth the climb, as once we completed the climb, we were met with a spectacular view of all of London set out below.

Within the walls of The British Museum is the historic library. This we saved for our final pass through. We wandered among the displays of historic papers, mystified. The library housed the Magna Carter,

Lewis Carroll's handwritten notes on Alice, and, magically, John Lennon's scribbled lyrics.

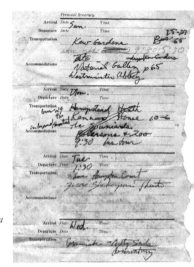

part of the itinerary that Gabriella and I set for the London trip

portfolio that Gabriella labeled and carried the Lennon film footage while on the plane to London

Chapter 20
The Live Auction

We arrived back home and a month later it was time for the Bonhams' auction. By then I had been assigned a Designer position in advertising at the newspaper, a day shift job. I planned time during my shift to watch the auction live! The computers at work provided a much better web connection than the one at home. Ted had sent the online links, which I had tested earlier in the week to ensure that I would be able to watch the transactions as they occurred in London. He had my contact phone number. Now, there was nothing to do but enjoy the auction.

As I sat at my desk, I marveled at how the computer age afforded me the immediate satisfaction of witnessing the live sale of my film halfway across the globe. The thrill of doing so was a groundbreaking moment for me.

With the link hooked up, and the Bonhams' catalog in my hand, one-by-one I could follow items as they came up on the auction block. For the past week I had calculated, over and over in my head, the conversion of British pounds to dollars and the potential amount the sale could fetch. Factoring in the time difference, Ted had also sent me an approximate time when I could expect my item to come up for sale and he had wanted my contact number in case there were further questions.

There I was, on February 18th, sitting at my work computer, logged on, the clock ticking. Item 914 was announced. My item would be next! Instead, item 916 brought up for bid. What? Where was item 915, my films? Did the computer skip something? My phone rang almost instantly. It was Ted.

"Yea, Ted it's me. What's going on?!! Where's my film?!!" I was frantic.

He said, "We have an issue."

I felt a coolness descend throughout my entire body, starting at my ears, as I listened to Ted's British accent explain what was going on.

"We have never had anything like this happen before." Ted continued. "I had to call the Bonhams owner in. Yoko's lawyers from EMI have come forward and stated that they own this film footage."

I started to explain, "No, they don't."

He assured me he did not believe them either, this was a tactic. "What happens now?"

Ted carefully explained that there were two options that his director recommended. If they, Bonhams, continued and placed the item on the auction block, the EMI lawyers could contest it. The film would be seized and would wind up in the British courts. British copyright laws, unlike the American laws, could tie up the litigation for years, and I would have to retain a lawyer to prove ownership.

God no! I could not believe what I was hearing.

Ted's second suggestion was better, as he admitted. "I don't care for

is kind of bullying. We have the option of not putting them up on
e auction block at all and sending them back to you. We would sim-
y say the seller has pulled this item from the auction. I will person-
ly assure you that I will get them back to you, Express Delivery."
The silence in my head was deafening, "Thank you, yes please send
em back, thank you Ted, thank you for everything you've done for
e."

Chapter 21
Studio One

The package arrived at my door by FedEx, just like Ted had promised. As I signed for it, I thought, Now what?

Meeting back with my coffee shop group, I let my frustration be known.

"I was so stunned and pissed! You can't imagine! These people think they own everything!"

Kevin, who had been listening from a different table said," I can sell them for you."

"What'd ya mean?" I asked.

"For a percentage of the profits, I'll sell them for you. Let me try."

Where else could I go? Why not? So, we agreed. He would get ten percent of the total take if he sold the films and ONLY the film. No t-shirts, prints, or posters. I did not want the EMI people after me now that they had me on their radar. And so, Kevin and I shook hands on it.

I was impressed that with a simple verbal agreement, and true to

Kevin's hustling nature, in just a few weeks he had managed to set up a meeting at Studio One. We were asked to come into New York City and meet with Yoko's lawyers and her archivist. We drove into New York City, an hour's drive from where we lived, Kevin, myself, and the reels of film still in the artist portfolio that had carried them for so long and so far.

As soon as we arrived, we were escorted by the receptionist to an enclosed room. There waiting for us was the lawyer, who was very much like most lawyers - suit, papers, pen at the ready, a basically non-descript person. It all seemed so tedious. We were introduced to Carmine, the archivist. She was much younger than I had expected, you could say she was a historian. Kevin did the introducing for us. The meeting was in a viewing room with equipment, screen, bottled water on the table, and a technician at the ready.

The conversation was polite. The lawyer directed questions to Kevin while I kept silent, listening and nodding. Kevin had made the arrangements, and as this was his gig, he did most of the talking. Our strategy was to reveal as little as possible about the circumstances surrounding my acquirement of the film.

I turned the film over to the projectionist. He seemed to be a nice guy; he handled the film like the prized item that it was. As he placed it into the slots for viewing, he commented that the film was in great shape, considering its age. He made some adjustments with the filters and said, "Look! All the color is still in there." He tweaked it again. "Whoever kept these knew something about film. There's no damage at all. Most of the time, film of this type loses its color because it's stored in the wrong environment." This was an accident of good fortune on my part, especially since I had stored them first in an extra refrigerator and then in the back of my closet.

The noise of the projector now sounded all too familiar to me. Eyes darted between the lawyer and Carmine, especially when they got a glimpse of May Pang in one sequence. The lawyer turned to Carmine when it finished and said," Have you ever seen these or any of this footage before?"

"No, I've never seen this footage."

"Me neither," he said.

Kevin and I played it cool and just glanced at each other.

After the viewing, the conversation was short, direct, and to the point. There was no small talk; this was business. "We'll need to get back to you. We need to speak with Yoko, of course."

"Of course."

The projectionist handed me the reels of film one by one, and as I started to zip up the portfolio getting ready to leave, he told me in a quiet voice, "Studio One is currently working on a documentary about John. Yoko is funding it."

The lawyer, who had been watching me as I packed up the reels, asked if he could have the film now to show it to Yoko. "Why don't you leave them with us? It will speed things up."

His tone was so patronizing, it was insulting. Loud and clear, in my head I heard the advice of my lawyer - 'owner's keepers'. Did this guy really think we were huckleberries from the backwoods of the Hudson Valley? Did he really think I was dumb enough to hand the film over to him just because I might be star struck? I stepped in and smiled and simply said, "NO, no thanks." Then I pulled out a section of the last reel of film and took the scissors off the desk. I clipped off six inches of frames and handed them to the lawyer. "But you can show her this."

Kevin was grinning, but then he said something stupid, REALLY stupid. It was his nature to always do one better, and this time he couldn't resist name-dropping. "You know I've also been in contact with Fred Seaman and discussed a possible deal." Of course, he was referring to the Fred Seaman who wrote the scathing book about John and Yoko.

Are you kidding me Kevin?

The lawyer turned to Carmine and said nothing more. He did not need to. His look of rage, vehemence, and ice was felt. His expression said it all.

We left with the film. All the way home, Kevin talked non-stop. He thought it had gone well, but I could not stop thinking about the look on the lawyer's face when Kevin mentioned Fred Seaman . Lousy Fred Seaman. Fred Seaman, whose book about John I had read earlier. Fred Seaman, with all his unscrupulous dealings, stealing and lies "WHY," I asked, would you think it was appropriate to associate us with Seaman?!!"

Kevin said I worried too much.

Chapter 22
The Pole Dancer

A week later a contract did arrive in the mail with a note to sign it and send it back. It was a basic sale contract. Listed on it was a decent price for the film and on the bottom were places for my signature and Yoko's, with our names typed underneath. According to the attached instructions, Yoko would sign the contract once I had signed and it and returned it. Kevin was ecstatic. Unfortunately, his elation would be short-lived.

After sending the contract with just my signature on it back to the lawyer, within days another letter arrived stating that Yoko had only agreed to sign it and pay just five thousand dollars for the film. This was nothing compared to the price that Bonhams had set and not even a third of what was offered in the first contract from Yoko's people.

"I knew it, I knew they didn't like the fact that you mentioned Seaman. They don't want to do business with us, and they don't trust us. Why did you bring him up!!?"

Kevin knew I was angry. I refused to sell the Lennon film for that diculously small amount, not after everything I had been through. Kevin made a final attempt to rectify the situation. He informed the lawyer that we were not selling for that price, but we were willing to negotiate. They never followed up with a counteroffer. In fact, we never heard from them again.

I told Kevin the deal with him was off, "I'm done with you." In my eyes Kevin and I had a verbal agreement for "when the film was sold." I had no intention of giving him anything. He had blown his opportunity, big time.

My association with Kevin had sent me back to nothing. Back to zero. Back to sitting at my desk.

At the time, the newspaper industry was going through a revolution. Technology was affecting major changes. Things were advancing so quickly, it was difficult to stay apace.

Across from the Design section was the Classified department. Everyone at the paper referred to the women who worked there as the 'classified gals.' Classified was the one department managed entirely by women.

Newspapers then were still a main source of information for most people, and the classified ads were an inexpensive place to place a blurb to buy or sell used appliances, furniture and cars. The classified ads were the place to look for job listings, apartment rentals, legal notices, and prior to internet dating services, people to hook up with. Ads were a way to announce anniversaries and weddings, graduations and birthdays, and local businesses regularly made themselves known with ads of varying size. The ads provided a steady and reliable source of revenue for the paper.

The phones never stopped ringing for the gals in Classified. They went day and night attached to their phones, taking orders and cold calling businesses. Their commissions depended on selling ad space.

To be on the safe side, the week following the debacle in NYC, I took out a classified legal ad terminating any business dealings I had had with Kevin.

Sharon was one of the gals in Classified. She was younger than most of the women who worked there. She was ambitious, thin-faced, long-haired, long-legged and well-endowed. She was well enough endowed to be a pole dancer, which is exactly what she had been. Prior to working in the Classified department, she had worked the pole at a local strip club. Yes, that is how she had earned a living before becoming a "classified gal," and she was proud of it! I liked her and often spent my lunch break talking with her over sandwiche

Sharon belonged to the generation that embraced everything com puters had to offer. In fact, she had convinced her boss that selling ads via the internet was the way to go for classifieds. The powers-that-be at the newspaper gave her a new position and moved her to the web department, which was still in its infancy. Her job was to explore the feasibility of selling online; her initial assignment to stuc eBay's system.

Come lunch break, Sharon would tell me all about eBay, giving me updates on the mechanics of how it worked. "It's a lot like an auc-tion," she would explain. She would take me to her workstation and pull up her screen. "Look. I put this item up for sale yesterday. I included some pictures, a description, lowest price and click. Anyon can do it."

"Can you sell stuff here on your own time? Do you think you could sell something for me?" I was hopeful.

I gave her an abridged version of my attempts to sell my film foot age of John Lennon. With the confidence of a gal who knew how t get a big tipper to tip even bigger, Sharon said, "Yea, I can sell it." V agreed to a ten percent commission just like any other sale she mad

Chapter 23
Sgt. Pepper

Back when I first had connections with Kevin, he had scanned some images from the film footage for me. He had a lot of equipment for his graphic business, including negative scanners. We had initially selected six images, all extracted from the different reels of film. Our intention was to provide a visual from the footage in correspondence with potential buyers.

I still had these in my computer files, and along with the information I had sent to Bonhams, Sharon and I had all the descriptive material needed to "go live" as she said. I watched as she downloaded the everything onto eBay. Then we waited. Sharon told me that sometimes people did not bid on an item till the final date of the sale. We needed to be patient, and if nobody bid, we could always try again. Within two days, Sharon said "Mare look. Someone's already bid on your item."

"Nice, what do we have to do?"

"We sit back and wait until the final bidding date has passed. We wait and see how high the bids get. Someone else can, and probably will, bid against this first bid."

"Cool."

Later that same day Sharon approached my desk with an unusual expression on her face.

"Man, I just got this contact message about your film."

Oh no! Please, no. My heart got that familiar sinking feeling it got when I received, or anticipated receiving, bad news.

Sharon began to explain, "There's this guy who contacted me. He's from California and says he's a huge Beatles collector. He tells me about all the stuff he has in his collection and says he's willing to go above the eBay asking price on one condition - he asks that we cease the online sale right now."

"What, what happens to the bid we already have?"

"Oh, no problem. We just ignore it, it was his bid!"

"Well yea!!!! Let's do it!" I cannot believe my ears are hearing this.

"Sit here, I'll call him now. Hey, get this -- his online username for his email is 'Sergeant Pepper.' Man, this guy is SERIOUS."

I was not going to get greedy. I just wanted my price, the tuition money for my daughter's college.

I spoke with Sergeant Pepper a couple of times; his real name was 'Bob.' I let Bob in on some of the particulars surrounding the film: how I had acquired it from a dumpster in New York City, the trip to Bonhams, what the Studio One technician had said. Bob said he could restore the footage. Each time we spoke, Bob would go on and on about the Beatles. I had to remind him that I was speaking from work, and time on the phone with personal calls was limited.

Finally, we settled on the details of the sale. Sergeant Pepper would become the sole owner of the films. As part of the arrangement, I even agreed to include the video copies. He would send a certified check, and as soon as I deposited it, I would send the films in an overnight insured package to California.

Part of me was sad to see the films go. They had been with me for so long. We had a history, but I knew that the new keeper was providing the right place for them, and overall, Sergeant Pepper was a good fit. Besides, he was paying big bucks, enough for me to cover my daughter' tuition.

After 27 years, I parted with the reels of John Lennon in a simple manner. There was none of the fanfare of a renowned auction house, none of the celebrity of Studio One. It was the infant days of eBay and the dawn of the decline of newspapers. I made a simple trip to the FedEx office, and off the films went, fully insured, to California.

Chapter 24
One Last Visit

Charlie and I did reunite eventually. Little did I know, we had both been seeking each other out. On an otherwise uneventful Saturday, the phone rang while cleaning the house.

"Mary, Mary, Mary do you know how hard it's been to find you? "

"Is this really you? I tried calling your old number, too. Your Dad said you were dead and hung up on me. I even found Joann and called her. She said she heard you were dead, too - a drug overdose. But I knew you were still alive. I had a dream that you were walking down the street laughing, your head held high, just laughing." Charlie laughed at that, and I pictured him grinning, head tilted like the Mad Hatter.

"Yea well, in my Dad's eyes I was dead, but I've been straight now for ten years, sober, no drugs, the works." We set up a meeting. It was rough to see the damage left by heroine. Three of his fingertips on his right hand had been amputated as the result of an overdose. He told me his guitar playing days were over after that episode. He now anged out his songs on a keyboard.

I eventually invited him up to visit. I wanted to introduce him to my Gabriella on one of her visits home, during her last year of college. Charlie came and asked me what happened to the Lennon films. He wanted to know if I still had them. I shook my head, 'No', and told him they had been sold. The money had paid for my daughter's education. He smiled, "Good."

When Gabriella graduated, it was without debt. Not one penny was owed for tuition, lodging, or books. Nothing. Thank you, John Lennon.

Charlie and I agreed to stay in touch. We visited on occasion. So much had separated us, and yet we were both still connected by our past adventures.

My daughter and I visited Charlie one last time. He was in the hospital. Charlie and I were in our fifties by then, and the drugs of his youth had aged him. He looked like he was eighty. He looked sunken and fatigued from surgeries. Bruises ran up and down his arms where IV hook-ups lingered. "Shit man," he said, "the one drug that's legal the one killing me - cigarettes." His internal organs did not function well under the stress of any illness.

Charlie is free now from the torment that had made him an easy target for drugs so many years earlier.

At Charlie's funeral, his Dad held me tight while he cried. "I still have that painting you did for Charlie," he said. "He loved it. He took it with him every time he moved."

"What painting?"

"The one you did of Gimbels department store."

I had completely forgotten about it. It was a Surrealist landscape using Gimbels as the focal point. Within the picture were the ele-

ments of our secret. Gimbels first opened its doors in 1887. In 198⁻
it ceased operations and closed its doors for good.

Ten years after selling my film, I found out that Sergeant Pepper had resold the film footage. An old friend from the coffee shop
called to tell me he saw that Christies had recently had a Rock' n Rol
auction. The online listing included the item - rare Lennon film foot
age. He thought I should know. It was the description of the same
footage I had once owned. It stated that the film had been initially
purchased from a young female film student in New York City. The
notice gave Christies' selling price; it was double the amount of wha
I had received from Sergeant Pepper.

"Aren't you angry about this? You could've gotten more," my
friend said.

"No, this guy deserves whatever he got for it. He took care of it
and I am sure he had to spend a lot to restore it. You know anything
on film is expensive. Besides, I got what I needed from it. I wish him
well." I could only speculate as to who the anonymous buyer was.

Last I heard, Kevin was up in the Catskills somewhere, close to
Woodstock. He was still selling t-shirts and prints and whatever els
he could wheel and deal. I also heard he was selling t-shirts with the
images of John Lennon, illegal images he had scanned for me so
many years back.

I hear from Steve, Charlie's sidekick. We used to call him Skip but
Steve is what he wants to be known as these days. He calls a few
times a year. Steve and Charlie had been like brothers. Steve calls
every New Year's Eve and on the anniversary of Charlie's death, Ma
4th. I also usually hear from him in late summer when he is going
to or coming back from the annual UFO Convention in Pine Bush,
New York. He likes to remind me, "You know babe, Pine Bush isn'

too far from where you live."

"I know, Steve." I never volunteer to meet up with him there, but I do enjoy hearing from him.

I last visited Steve in Yonkers, shortly after Charlie died. Steve was then, and still is, living in his studio apartment, just a few blocks from the old neighborhood that he grew up in. It is at the cross section of Yonkers and the Bronx, close to Gun Hill Road. His place is cluttered and stacked floor to ceiling with books, tapes, and vinyl records, with barely enough room to walk through the piles. He told me he had been there for decades. I believed him; it certainly looked that way. Steve survives on disability for God knows what - depression, arthritis, whatever non-functioning people get classified, in order to stay alive.

I do not mind his phone calls. They are a little reminder of my friend Charlie.

I tell Steve about how I am still painting and using my talent for creative organizing to put together fundraising events for local non-profit art groups, as well as my town's historical society. I tell Steve that the rebel in me is still alive and well, as I'm always badgering the village board, concerning one thing or another that I feel needs to be addressed. I look forward to Steve's calls. I am always glad to talk with him, and I wonder who, if anyone, will call me to tell me when he has finally taken off.

My phone rings. It is Steve. He starts with his rants about this year's convention in Pine Bush. "You know, babe, they walk among us."

"Who, Steve, who are you talking about? Who walks among us?"

"Aliens man, aliens."

The End

online announcement of second auction for the "unseen" Lennon film.

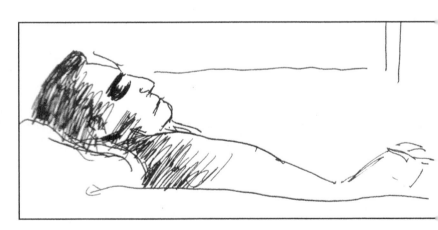

drawing of Charlie dead in his coffin at his funeral 2005

The Gimbels painting done in 1973 only recently discovered hanging in Steve's apartment in Yonkers behind a floor to ceiling stack of CD's. The painting was given to him by Charlies father after his death.

About the Author

Mary Altobelli is an artist/activist involved in civic and environ-ental affairs. As an artist she expresses herself with bold colors. Her ain medium is oil painting and she has an affinity for the woodcut ock printing process as well as watercolor. Mary has written and ustrated several zines with her woodcuts.

Mary infuses her subjects with a sense of empathy and joy that e brings to all forms of expression. "As a creative person, I am ways inspired by a sense of place whether artistically in painting or the telling of a story." www.maryaltobelli.com

Made in the USA
Monee, IL
15 May 2021